Nobody
Ever Told Me...

By
Michelle Elizabeth Williams

CHAPTER I

It's a Crazy Life

If God can change me, he can change anyone....

It all started when I was just a little girl. My first memory of abuse is of the babysitter sitting on me and covering my nose and mouth after slapping me in the face. "Shut up," she said, as the tears rolled down my face and onto her clutching hand. "If you tell your mother, I'll do it again." At that tender age, I knew if I told my mother she would never do it again—so I told.

One thing I've come to realize about life is that I was never prepared for all the unseen things that I was going to have to feel my way through. Life gets funny. Sometimes it's challenging and unpredictable, sometimes it's up and sometimes down, and you really don't know what's going to happen from one day to the next even though you try to prepare, You hope with great expectancy every day you wake up and look forward to get to know the new day better than the day before. You wonder if life will make you laugh today or make you cry. Often you can have steady situations, but what happens when the unthinkable approaches and you are unprepared? Who's to say that life is fair? (Life has a way of making you say amen after the curve ball is thrown into your back yard instead in the ballpark) (T.D Jakes)

Why Me!!!

I remember being five when a neighbor came over to my yard and picked me up and put me on a tree. He pulled my little dress up and I remember seeing something milky colored white.

"What's that?" I asked.

"That's milk," he replied.

He later came back to do this thing to me a second time, but my older brother, who was six, ran and told that a guy had me on a tree. I knew he told because when I was approaching the steps of my house, I heard him telling what he had seen. And he was totally correct; I could not have told it any better. (To my late brother: Thanks, Snooky!)

Wow! What a tear jerker after all these years. I never knew that I would be so grateful to someone for tattle tailing on me; after that episode it never happened again—well, not with him anyway. I can still remember the look on my mother's face.

"Did he hurt you?" she asked. I said no, because in all honesty I didn't remember him hurting me. He didn't penetrate me, but he did violate me. This thing that he did to me would change my life forever. In hindsight, I shut down for quite a while.

Anyway, my mother marched me right across the street, holding my hand, and we went to the perpetrator's house. I can clearly remember his mother's face, like, "What did he do now?" I was scared, because I felt my mother hurting and boiling at the same time. Maybe it was because of all those choice words that she was using that I was not allowed to use. As I stood there, my mom said, "Tell her what he did to you and tell her what he said about the milk."

By then my mother was just totally disgusted. I could tell in her eyes and in her voice. Even though she was standing with me, when I began to reveal what had happened to me, I felt like I was standing alone. Something that was supposed to be a beautiful experience now was being shattered in a few words of regret.

I had to become an advocate for myself. As I began to tell his mother, I felt tall within, like, "I can face this mountain." Looking back, I see a little girl with her finger in her mouth and twisting her right foot, but still telling everything that he had done. I don't remember being loved or shown any type of affection or compassion, like a hug or something. I do remember the mother of the guy saying that she was sorry.

Finally we left her house. When we returned to our house, my mom demanded, "Why you didn't tell me?" She was hollering and I felt like she was hollering at me, but I now know from being a parent myself that she was just angry about the situation and probably mad that she couldn't protect me from what I call the big bad wolf.

Although that is my last memory of the situation, something else began to happen to me: I started hating milk. I didn't want it in my cereal and I would never ever drink it plain. Something that took less than five minutes changed my whole perception of life. They say that milk is good for you, but the milk that I experienced made my mom sad, made me uncomfortable and it made the mom of the guy who molested me hold her head in shame. I would see TV commercials with kids with huge smiles on their faces in front of a bowl of cereal or a tall glass of milk, and I was totally confused. Was I supposed to be happy about the milk or be ashamed of it? I didn't know what to do at that early age but as life progressed and I began to learn the difference between good and bad, I was able to let go of that baggage. I grew up lactose intolerant, so that helped quite a bit in my healing.

I realize something special now that I am older:

To my late mom: Thanks for holding my hand throughout the situation. Maybe at that time I stood tall because you were there with me and I wasn't all alone after all. Thanks for your helping hand that led me into the strong independent young lady that I am today. What you did for me that day was help me face my problems head on. And you never took me to the bad guy; you took me to someone who had more authority than him—his mother. You showed me at an early age how to do things right away. Mom, you did the best that you knew how. Daughters, Sons, Nieces and nephews and cousins always tell if someone has touched you, make sure you tell someone that you can trust that can protect you. 1. If someone touches you in any way that makes you feel uncomfortable tell. 2. If it's someone that you trust that touches you then tell another person that you trust because everyone will not hurt you. 3. At times people won't believe you because they are afraid of what may happen to the other person that has touched you but still tell because they actually do believe you they just don't know how to deal with the situation so the easiest thing to do is go into denial, this is something that this person has done before and most people know it except for you. 4. You will hurt from the betrayal and you may even blame yourself and say I made them do this to me but it's not your fault. 5. Again don't blame yourself. 6. At times when being molested it doesn't hurt it actually may feel good if someone is rubbing you in those sensitive places, and that's why some of us allow it to continue? 7. It's a violation of the adult that does this to you and throw you into early sexual stimulation that makes you either become promiscuous (very sexually active) or makes you master bait to achieve the feeling over and over again. The sin is that they took you there when you were not ready. 8. You must take control over your life and forgive those that hurt or betrayed you. The reason that you must do this is because it will eat you alive as you become older. It happened to me and it ate me alive with a hatred that hurt me more than it hurt him. He lived his life just like nothing ever happened and I suffered in silence for years. It will create bitterness in you and you will not have a full life while carrying it especially when it has turned into rape or something violent. I allowed God to help heal me and I finally forgave them. 9. I turned it all over to God and he healed me from the inside out, I found a real person to trust that could truly pray with me to achieve my deliverance. 10. Begin to tell your story and don't hold it in. You don't have to be ashamed of what someone did to you they are the ones that need to be ashamed. Free yourself and others by telling your story. Release yourself from the pain and the shame. It's not your fault. Now be free.

Now looking back, I can see and find the good things that you showed me from something that was supposed to destroy me. Thanks, Mom, I will always love you for that.

Love, your daughter always,

Missy

My Dad

My dad was quite the Dr. Jekyll and Mr. Hyde. He drank—almost all the time. I used to stare at my dad when he was sober and think to myself that he was the nicest person in the whole wide world. When he was sober he never raised his hand to hit me and he never even swore. I thought, "Wow, what a nice guy." But my brother and I hated when we sat and watched the western show on television with him. I would turn and see my father taking sips of the bottle that made him turn into an evil man that I didn't even recognize. God, was he different! I couldn't understand how this could happen, and happen so quickly.

The memory is so vivid that it is sickening. I would turn to peek at him as slyly as possible because I didn't want to upset him. Any little thing would set him off and make him beat me. As I watched him, I felt like a new man was coming up and out of my father. It always amazed me that people could change like that, and so quickly. Wow! As the new man began to appear, I would stare at the TV like I was really into it. I would notice his voice going from full and natural to slurring and out-of-control. From my side view I would notice him getting up and leaning from side to side. His voice would become angrier and he would begin to get louder and louder. I've never understood why people get loud when they drink. It's not like the rest of us are deaf and can't hear them. And I could never understand how a nice person could be so mean.

In all honesty, I saw the drunken side of my father more than I saw anything else. I went to bars with him at a young age. There were some fun times when he would give me a quarter to play my favorite tune or he would let me play pool with him. That was kind of nice. It wasn't the greatest, but it was better than the rest of my time with him.

I hated watching my father get into an argument with other men at the bar, though. After about a few minutes, it would turn into a fight, then rolling on the floor. Next thing you know, I saw my father being punched in the face, and then I saw him hit another guy—and he was so drunk he could barely stand up. I was so young and I felt so guilty because I couldn't help my dad. He would get up bloody, and I was so scared that I think that I internalized these events to where even now I don't like the sight of blood. As a matter of fact, I get so bad when it comes to blood that I feel like passing out. Perhaps I hate blood the way that I do because of my wild and crazy childhood.

I never realized how much pain the situation with my dad has caused me. It was something that I needed to bring out so I could pray on it. I need deliverance from the fear that I've been carrying for years. I hate blood and I hate brawls. I hated the brawling because sometimes my dad would come home from the bar and have to sit in the tub with his face looking dismantled. He never knew how badly he had been beaten until the next day. God it was so sad the next day when he wasn't the evil man anymore and he was the nice guy. I hated seeing the nice guy all beat up.

I never liked to see my mom upset over my dad's drinking. It was not the best life for her or for us children to endure. I never really had any good days at school because of my dad's alcohol problem. It wasn't a casual thing, it was an everyday thing. And I mean every day. I hated to see the police coming to our house, but on the other hand it always stopped the fighting. At least my mom was able to get herself together and have him stop harassing and hitting her. I never knew it until she told me later, but when I was beaten as a child, a woman by the name of Elder Sandra Hopgood would sometimes call the police and that would stop the beating. I give thanks to all who called the police to help save us children from this affliction in our lives.

You want to hear something kind of crazy? My dad was the real comedian of the block. He would always be outside cracking jokes and keeping everyone laughing and he would even buy the children of the area ice cream. At the time I thought that he was pretty nice. It wasn't like I had lots of friends, and everyone always talked bad about our family because of our drunken father. So when he bought ice cream for everyone, it wasn't all that bad because just for that moment, my dad was the greatest, and there was not one mean word being said. He bought ice cream quite often, even while he was drunk. It wasn't always bad, but on the other hand, it wasn't the greatest either.

Another good time was when my father would take all the change out of his pocket and throw it in the middle of the living room floor for all of us kids to get. If you got a quarter in those days, it almost felt like you received a million dollars because there was a little store called Ms. Dee's where candy was a penny. Whenever I found even a nickel on the ground, I would go to the store because candy to me was just candy. No matter how many, I was happy. It never took much to make me happy, just the little things. I mean that from the bottom of my heart. Cavities ran very prevalent at that time in my mouth. The dentist must have been happy to see me. I was seeing penny candy and he was seeing dollar bills.

Now that I am older, I can honestly say that I am a survivor of abuse by an alcoholic.

CHAPTER 2

My Bleeding Heart

There was a time that I thought that no one could ever love me. As a child I went through many obstacles that made me feel loveless. As a child I always felt in my heart that someone somewhere would love me—but whom? I went on a journey in search of love. Not just to be in love, but to be loved as an individual person. Eventually I found it, never knowing that love lived in me. If I had made better choices in life, love would have prevailed a lot sooner. The scars on my skin go much deeper than the visual appearance of the hurt that I had to endure. They provoked the pain that lies deep within the depths of my being. Every time they began to hurt, I could feel my insides scream. Welts of a lifetime grew inside me, and every time things didn't go right for me. I would feel it all over again, just like it was yesterday. I remembered what everyone had done to me and how they did it. Yes, it was hard for me to let it go.

Before I knew it, I had another person living inside of me, and I had to get rid of the person that now tried to ruin my life. That person was me. No, I am not saying that what happened to me was my fault, but the bad choices I made landed me into an even deeper ditch. I was in trouble and I needed help.

I didn't know then that I was my own worst enemy. In my thoughts, in my actions, and in my life, I ran for cover, but I ended up in the dry desert and the only place for refuge in my desert was the cactus tree. It hurt me, it stung me and it even made me bleed, but I got my freedom through the blood of my pain. It forced me to tear off the very thing that had held me back from me. The blood was seeping through my clothes. It covered me with grief. I was stricken with dirt. When help came to rescue me, the only way I could be seen was through the blood that was on my shirt, that ripped through my body. My rescuers saw my hurt, they saw my pain, and when they saw the wave of my bloody garment, I was taken up away from the dirt, cactus and blood.

My healing began to take place when I opened up and let people see the stains of my blood. As I was being airlifted through the past hurts of my life, I felt blood dripping from my heart, and the higher I got the less the drips became. Before I knew it, the freshness of the air started to dry up the open patch that needed healing. Oh, yes, I was wounded. Not only was I wounded, but my soul was torn and my spirit was ripped, but yet and still, God saw fit to give me a real chance at life and I found life through his love. I couldn't believe it. God loved me. Why? I had questions and he had answers, I had doubts but he had belief, I had scars but he was the surgeon that fixed me up in the operating room. I walked away and he waited patiently for me. I broke his heart, but he still mended mine.

Finally, with his arms open wide, he called me again, and this time I came running, And God spoke these very words to me, "I love you and I am the lover of your soul."

I said, "What, God?"

And he said it again, "I love you. I am the lover of your soul and I care for you."

I broke down and cried, and in the midst of my tears, he said, "I want you to find love, joy, peace and happiness in me, and when a good man does enter into your life, he will be an asset to our love."

Before I knew it I was swept off of my feet by God. He began to woo me. I have never had a love like that nor will I ever find any like it. God's love is like no other. Even when I walked away from him; I still couldn't find any love that compared. I love God with all of my heart, and with my every waking breath, I am thanking him for life.

Why Was I So Jealous?

I never thought or even imagined waking up one morning and saying to myself, "I think I'll be jealous today." I mean, most kids say they want to be a doctor, a lawyer, a nurse or something special. I couldn't believe I was so jealous. I began digging deep into myself and I found out the reason when and why I was the way that I was.

It all started out when I pulled out a picture of myself of when I was about nine and a half, and saw myself as a child with the biggest smile. I hadn't known then that what I was going through was abuse, and I was still a happy person on the inside. I didn't realize that this thing called jealousy was going to rise up and take root inside and then begin to control me and take charge. I've never understood how something so small could turn into something so big and captivate me to where I was ready to pull a gun if need be. How could it be that I was ready to drag a woman by her hair with one hand and beat her in her face with my other hand while I was in church?

Oops, did I say church? Yes, I did. It never actually happened but the thoughts ran through my head so much that it may as well have happened. There came a point when I needed to deal with this spirit before it dealt with me. It was definitely time for this bitter tree to be dug up by the root and burned. If I didn't allow this thing to die in my life, I was going to have to be a lonely camper for the rest of my days, even while in a relationship. It was not just one woman who was the object of my jealousy; it was any woman that got next to my territory. I felt like a predator not looking for a prey, but if she just happened to stray into my path like a prey does, then me, being the apex wolf or mama lion, would have to take her down like a vulture.

How could all this anger and resentment be coming from someone like me who really loved God? I was singing on the choir, working with hurting children, helping others with their bad situations, but I was being eaten alive like a carcass. I want to take you through a journey of my childhood life to show you how I got from A-Z of a lifetime of jealousy that was sown as a seed.

The Journey

Here I was, this sweet little girl with deep eyes, deep dimples and always in deep thought about how, when I grew up, I would have the nicest clothes in the whole wide world. Hand me downs were all I received. They covered my back and kept me warm, but they were ugly and dingy. Yes, they were a blessing in disguise, but given the way those clothes looked, I would rather have been in disguise! As a child, these things hurt my little girlish ego and pride. My daydream was to wear a three-piece suit, then called gauchos, but today might be called culottes.

Here was the very first seed of jealousy planted in me. I went to school with another little girl named Vickie Lee. She often came to school in those little suits that I desired to have. Not only that, she was very pretty. On day she came in a pair of pink pants, a white shirt, a crisp pair of white sneakers, and a pink headband with her hair pulled back in a neat ponytail. I stared at her the whole day. Her clothes and her neatness became my desire. I used to say I wanted to be like Vicki Lee when I grew up. The kids teased me so much that I desired to look like her too.

I had childhood daydreams in school and at home in which I wildly imagined that she would pass all her hand me- downs on to me because I would have worn them with pleasure. I felt since everyone else passed down their old dirty clothes, why not get her beautiful clothes. Everybody stared at Vicki. She was like today's Top Model. Even at that early age, she made me want to better myself through nice clothes.

One day my mom received a bag of clothes for me from a neighbor. I was always excited to see what I had gotten because I thought one day I would get something from Vicki.

That never happened, but to my surprise, my neighbor Tami Costello blessed me with some pretty little dresses and a beautiful pair of white pants that fit my little 10-year-old shape perfectly. I couldn't wait to go to school and show off my new clothes. Tami gave me as many shirts, pants and everything that a girl could ever want that would fit into one bag.

I never did get my gauchos, but what I did receive changed my life. I tried to wear my new white pants every day. Of course mom wouldn't let me. I would go to school in my new dress and come home and take that off and put on my white pants and walk around my room looking at myself in the mirror. I was so happy. I was the happiest abused little girl in the Rondout Gardens complex. Tami really made a difference in my life; she bought the sunshine out of me when skies were gray. Just as bad things take root in your life and you never forget them, good things do the same and make quite an impact. Her gift of clothes led me to help the less fortunate with nice things to change their lives.

Mom Cuts My Hair Off

Another life-changing experience, besides being teased for my dingy hand-me-downs or having a drunk for a dad, was at the age of nine when my mother shaved off all of my hair and sent me to school the very next day. The adult neighbors couldn't believe it; they were coming over to see my head while I was sitting in the bathtub taking a bath. I would wear a scarf every day so that no one would know, but one day while I was in the process of waiting for my hair to grow back, I went to the Rondout Neighborhood Center to play and a little girl by the name of Phyllis pulled my scarf off. The expression on her face was of shock. She had her hand over her mouth, but the laugh seeped out through her fingers. Then she ran off screaming and laughing. I tried to hide in the janitor's closet, but he came in and saw me crying and said I had to get out of there. I stood still; I couldn't move, still crying.

He said softly, "Come on now," but before he could comfort me, all the other children came running and laughed at me. There were a couple that didn't laugh because they were in shock. The janitor told the children, "Get out of here! You've seen enough. Move!" The kids began to leave one by one. I stayed there until every child left and I was clear to go. I went home, crying all the way in anger, shame, and embarrassment.

After crying myself to sleep and waking up from a long night's rest, I got up with a new attitude. I decided that I was kind of glad that the news about my bald head was out because I was tired of the pressure of someone eventually finding out. I figured it was OK I was already used to being teased, so "bald head" would just be another name added to the list. Not long after, the center held a parade and they needed an Indian. I boldly asked them, "Can I be your bald little Indian?" and to my surprise they said yes. They made an Indian chief hat for my head and I rode the float like a champion, sitting at the top where all could see me. I had the biggest smile on my face because I felt as if I fit into something that felt wonderful. I waved at the crowd like I was Miss America and the crowd waved back with cheers. You know what they say: What the devil meant for evil God meant for your good.

Nina

After all of that, I met a lady by the name of Nina Mapes, who was very pretty and she dressed elegantly. Anytime she would see me down in my neighborhood, she would wave and say, "Hi, Cutie." I would think, "She isn't talking to me, is she? Nah, not her." I thought she was too pretty to call me cute, but she insisted that I was cute, and for years she called me "Cutie" or "Dimples." I liked that so much that I began going by her job at the Key Bank on my way to the YMCA just to say hello and to have her wave and make me feel whole and alive.

She always had something nice to say to me and I thrived off her kind words. So many negative things were being thrown at me by others, that I began to feel I was being stoned. In the midst of all the mean words, there was one small voice that threw my life into a whirlwind and made me feel I could fight the world with some kindness. It wasn't that I felt cute because I didn't. It was just that someone took time for me, and she called me "Cutie" and "Dimples" with a beautiful smile on her face that said she was sincere. I don't know if Nina will ever truly understand what she did for me because such kindness comes to her naturally, but I will always be grateful and appreciative for the two kind little words she spoke to me. They will always ring in my heart and mind. I will always be grateful to her for instilling those words in me. It's the little things that really mean a lot.

To Nina: I never told you this, but you helped me want to become more ladylike too. I used to see how neat you were. I looked at the wristwatches that you wore and the rings on your fingers and your nice attire, and it made me want to be just like you. I grew up from the age of ten not wanting to be a tomboy anymore because I figured that if I wanted to be a lady, I had to wear a watch and a ring. Your wrists and hands had to look pretty so you could be a lady. The funny thing is every time I go to buy a bracelet or I see a watch, I think of you and I still want to wear them so I can look like a lady. What an impact you had on my life! I just want to say that you were and still are so ladylike. Thank you, Nina.

Mom's Girlfriends

I began watching things that I probably shouldn't have seen but did. I was bound to the house like a slave. I had to mop floors, clean bathrooms, separate the colored clothes from the white for eight people in the house, and wash dishes three times a day with the double sinks filled up all three times. When they made the movie, Cinderella, they really meant to put my name down.

I played that role extremely well. I was very angry that I had to handle every household chore without a murmur. I better not say a word or I would be wearing my teeth on the back of my head like a ponytail wrapper, or they would be down my throat or on the floor.

I sure didn't want to give my parents a reason to beat me.

They already thought they had reason enough. My sisters were very spoiled. They got popped every once in a while, but nothing compared to me. I couldn't figure it out. Why me? I took care of everything for my mom. Couldn't she see it? Didn't she see it was me?

I was also mad because not only did we have our own household, we often had others. My mother's friends would come over and live with us a while with their five children. Time and time again, Mom would take in all these people. She was a person that didn't want to be alone so she always had one, two or three of her friends over. After a while her friends would come over while mom was at work. They were so much a part of the family that no one really minded. It got to the point where they wouldn't even knock. When Mom was home, she always seemed very happy having them around. They always laughed and joked and had a good time. I never saw any of them fight. Mom was there for them when they cried or went through evictions. She even helped them when they had men problems. Mom was there to rescue them. Since her friends had kids, we always had someone's child or children living under our roof. It was a lot of fun having other kids around because it made things less boring, but the dishes were killing me.

One day while Mom was at work, I saw my dad touching one of her friends that lived with us the wrong way. She seemed to like it because she didn't tell him to stop. After about five or ten minutes with them not knowing I was watching, they walked past me in the living room and she said, "Me and your dad are going in here. Be good and watch TV. OK?"

I didn't say a word. I was not stupid. They went in there and did the nasty and finished up just before Mom got home. When she came in from a hard day's work, her friend was all in her face smiling and talking to her like she had not done something earlier with my mom's husband. It always hurt me to hear her close friend say Hey Ruthie, right after she slept with my father as she came in from a hard day's work.

Mom continued being her friend and she kept coming over to our house and sleeping in my mom's bed with my father, even after she got her own apartment. Mom just didn't know what was going on. She was in the dark.

Another time while Mom was at work and this lady came over, my brother and I were sitting on the living room floor and she sat right on the couch and put her mouth on my drunk father's private parts. When we turned around to see what was going on, she said, "Turn around. I am just taking good care of your father."

My brother and I just looked at each other and turned back around and watched the television, and within two or three minutes, before the lady could get finished, my father was snoring. He was too drunk to do anything.

As time progressed, my dad slept with a few of my mom's friends. Since I was always forced to stay home, I heard all the gossip that was going on. I didn't know about there were so many until one day when he came in drunk and was fussing with everyone in the house and blurted out to one of the ladies, "Oh, just shut up. That why you gave me a blow job last night?" He even went on to say how good it felt to him because she didn't have any teeth. Boy, did she get up and go into a rage! "That's a lie!" she said. "I would never do that to Ruthie!" I thought in my head, "Sure. That's why I saw my father feeling all over your breast, and with his hands all over you." That's when Mom found out what kind of friends she had, and boy, was she mad!

One bad result of this was that later on in my life when my friend's sister betrayed me and slept with my kid's father while I was pregnant, it stirred up a good deal of anger and jealousy toward women in general. I still hadn't recognized that it stemmed from this. I didn't realize that these experiences had taken a bitter root inside of my spirit. I didn't know that women could be so ruthless and cold toward one another and still stand in their face and say, "I love you." I felt that what they did to my mother was dirty and I was so afraid to tell. I didn't know how much this had affected me until my pastor brought it to my attention. I didn't know this was something I was holding inside and I never forgave these people who hurt my mother. I carried it so deep inside that when I sensed a woman trying to use influence to get close to any man that was taken. I would get very upset and offended. I had to call out each woman's name and tell God that I forgave them. I had to let it go. The one time I did get up the nerve to tell on my father was when he was trying to kiss one of our family friends. At the time Mom had a secret boyfriend, but still the woman that he was touching was very uncomfortable and she begged me to tell my mom because she didn't want my mom to think that it was her. The whole ordeal happened because my father was drunk. I told Mom, and she wanted to leave anyway, so she packed her bags and moved in with the man that she had living in our house right with my father living there, too.

When dad got home he leaned over me on the couch and said, "You opened your big mouth and told your mother about me trying to kiss that girl." I said nothing at all. "Now your mother has left me because of you," he continued. "You made your mother leave me because of your big—," and before I knew it he punched me in the face. At the time, I was fourteen. My dad leaned up and went into the bedroom and fell asleep immediately.

I got up and I told my brother, "Today is the last day that I let that him put his hands on me." Quite honestly, I didn't say it that nicely. I called him every son-of-something that I could. I was tired and fed up by now. I told my brother, "Either you stay here with him or you come with me." I packed my bags and my brother came with me for the first day, but he wanted to go back to my father. I thought, oh well. As long as I was out, I didn't care.

I hated the fact that our whole family was split up. Mom had been moving in and out, back and forth, for some time. Finally when she did return home, my dad did one last thing that broke off the relationship for good. I had come back home for a short period. Anything had to be better than this. Anyway, my brother was sitting on the step in the house, I had just been beaten for something or another, I don't remember what. My father said something to my brother and he must have said something back that my father didn't like. My father picked up a vase and threw it at my brother's head. He only missed because of my brother's quick move. The big vase busted all over the wall. That's when Mom said "That's enough." From that day on my dad never lived in the house again. I was angry, hurt and mad because I felt, "Why did it take a vase thrown at my brother to get my dad out? What about me?" I felt like she could have done more for me and that's where more jealousy came in.

CHAPTER 3

Mom Left Me Behind

When mom decided to get up and leave us, I was just a little curious why she would leave my brother and me with an abusive alcoholic. If you leave your husband, you take all of your children. I came home from school one day and found to my surprise that Mom had left and taken my three little sisters with her. She didn't even say goodbye to me. It felt empty in that big house without noise, cooking or fighting. Quiet was not what I was used to. At first my father was upset. Then he decided that he was going to try to forget her, saying we would be just fine without her.

After a few days and she didn't come home or even call us, my dad got drunk and took us to where my mother was staying with her new boyfriend. I got very excited as I really wanted to go and see my mother. I missed her. It seemed to me that life was not fun without my unstable family. We pulled up in the yard and my father began blowing his horn. He started hollering, "Ruthie, come out here!"

We waited but that didn't work so he let me get out of the car to go knock on the window. My pleasure, I thought. Here was my chance to get away from my drunken father and be with my mother. I got out of the car and I ran to the window as fast as possible and I could see my mom.

I said, "Hi, Mommy," feeling so happy inside. "Daddy wants you."

"No," she replied. "I am not coming out."

I didn't care if she came out or not as long as I could go in and stay with my mom.

"Mommy, open the window," I said.

She said no.

"Mommy, can I please stay here with you?" I asked.

"No," she said. "Go with your father."

"Mommy, please can I please stay with you," I begged. "I don't want to go back with Daddy."

She told me to go with my father and walked away from the window without saying goodbye or anything. After a minute or two, I walked away from the window feeling very low. The woman that bore me didn't even have enough love for me to take me with her. She allowed me to stand there and cry and beg her to let me in and she wouldn't even open the window.

Out of all of the beatings and all the things that she and my father had done to me, I felt like this was the worst. I expected horrible things from my dad because he was an alcoholic, but my mom? No, never. I thought that she would be my protector, but she allowed me to go home to endure more beatings.

I guess I shouldn't be so mad at her because she had really had enough. The man she was dating made her feel really special. This time for sure my mother was happy. I had never seen her smile as much as she smiled with him. She always spoke very highly of him and I always thought of him as wonderful for the couple of years that I knew him—until he said something that offended me.

My friend and I often played wrestling and he would join in sometimes. I never thought anything of it because he was my mom's man. One day we were playing our wrestling moves and he started tickling me and making me laugh out loud. We were having lots of fun—or so I thought. I finally have a dad who wanted to love me and treat me the way a daughter was supposed to be treated. As we played together, I heard him say, "I want some of that."

"Some of what?" I asked, and he pointed at my private parts. I thought to myself, "No way, not him!" He walked away and I dismissed it as though it never happened because I was good at doing that. I figured if I stopped playing and laughing with him so much, he would dismiss it, too. Then about a month later he came up to me and started laughing and playing again. I tried not to think anything of it. I was a forgiving person, and he had never really done anything out of the way besides saying what he said, which to me didn't make him the worst person in the world. I laughed at him and he seemed relieved that I would laugh with him again. I figured he knew that he offended me once and that he would not do it again. I believed he'd learned his lesson.

We went back to our normal times, laughing and tickling and playing like father and daughter would do—until he was walking in front of me going up the stairs and I was walking behind him on my way up to the living room. All I remember is that he had these big hands and he was about six-foot-six. I continued walking behind him laughing until he was on the third or fourth step. As I stepped up onto the step, I looked up and saw this big hand coming toward me. He reached down and put a tight grip on me right between my legs, grabbing my vagina and holding it very tightly. It seemed like slow motion. I still hear him laughing as he held on to my private parts. I tried pushing his hand off and then pulled back to get away from his grip.

Finally he let go. I stared at him with this look of violation. I knew that I could never trust him again. From that time on, I never looked at him again and I never spoke another word to him ever. I never told my mom because she loved him so much, and she had already been through enough with my father's unfaithfulness. I didn't want to be the one to make her cry, so I carried the weight of heaviness for my mother. It always hurt me that the love of Mom's life would do that to me, but the sad thing was I never even saw it coming. Shortly after that I moved out to begin life on my own.

Look at Me

God look at me
Tell me what it is that you see is
When I look at you
I see a king
When I look at you
I see a queen
God look at me
Please tell me
What is it that you see?
When I look at you
I see pure beauty

When I look at you
I see me
Oh my child
When I look at you
I see me!!!!
But God
How can you see, you in me
When you look at me
How?
How can you see beauty?
As this wretch that I am
What makes you see something?
Good within my soul
How can you love someone like me?
When my rottenness is so old
What is it that you see?
Oh God when you look at me
Please God tell me
What is it that you see?
When you see me
God says
Oh my child
I see wonders
When I see you
I see perfectness and wholeness
When I see you
Oh child when I see you
I see my son
And child, I remember
All that he had done
So child
He did it for you
As well as he did it for me
So when you ask me
What is it that I see?
When I see you

I tell you that
I see me
When I see you
I see me
In the beginning I saw dust
I added a soul and a spirit
And I knew that you were a must
I know that you got dirty
As dirty as mud
But because you came back to me
All I see when I see you
Is my Son's precious blood
And God says
And that's enough for me.

CHAPTER 4

Memories

I wanted to believe in myself. I didn't like myself or my body. Nothing was wrong with it, but because of abuse, my mind fell into the trap of low self esteem. I even hated the dimples in my face. I would sit in school and whisper a silent cry asking why these holes were in my face. Maybe I wasn't ugly at all. Maybe not all that attractive, but certainly not the ugly child I was made to feel to be.

One time I was standing outside in the area where I lived minding my little business and two women were there. One of them said to me in improper English, "You must going to be real pretty when you grow up," and her friend asked her, Why did you say it like that?" As they walked off, she replied, "Because she sure is ugly now!"

I stood there in a state of shock. I knew in my heart that the words that she had just spoken were evil and whether she knew it or not, she had just bought death to my spirit. She had wounded me and left me there to bleed. I was already feeling bad about Mom cutting my hair because the perm had caused my nice hair to break off. She felt if she shaved my head that my new hair would have a better chance at growing in healthier.

Actually Mom had cutting fever. She would cut anything that wasn't tied or nailed down. She even cut my little sister's hair, so I actually couldn't take that personally, but as a child I did. Honestly, Mom messed up my hair long before I was nine. She gave me a perm because I had these four thick ponytails that she considered too nappy for her to deal with. She gave me a perm with lye in it. Back then, they didn't have perms without lye. When mom put the perm in my hair, she sat me in the bathtub with my little brother. While the perm was working, she and Dad got into an argument that quickly escalated into a fistfight and all I could hear was vulgar language and things being banged around and falling.

In the meantime, I was in the tub screaming because my head was burning from the perm that needed to be washed out. If I remember correctly, my eyes were burning too, but I wasn't sure whether it was from the perm or from the soap in my eyes from rubbing them while I cried. I was in excruciating pain. My scream was the only movement that took place, and that was the last thing I remember. I must have blocked the rest out. When I visualize this event, all I can see is a little child of four or five sitting in the tub as straight as possible screaming with everything in her. Now I can see myself just as though I am looking at someone else, but all along, it was me.

There was another episode, an attack on my hand, that I believe happened to try to stop my writing skills. I was in the back seat of my dad's moving black Cadillac on the passenger side. I don't know how it happened, but my door wasn't all the way closed and before I knew it, I was swinging out of the car and my fingers got caught up in the door and one almost ripped off. I couldn't hold on to the swinging car door any longer and I remember rolling and rolling over by the guardrail. I don't know if I passed out or not, but I remember seeing a yellow and black guardrail over my face as I looked up. As I looked down, it appeared to be a small bridge site and I was thinking I could fall through its cracks.

The yellow guardrail played over and over in my head and in my dreams, until it paralyzed me so that I couldn't drive over bridges without having an anxiety attack. It wouldn't matter if there was water under it or not, I was still afraid. Someone would have to hold my hand for me to have to cross but I am in a much better place now. In my mind I am still a little afraid of the bridge thing but I just take long deep breaths and tell myself I am bigger than this situation and it no longer has control over me, I have control over it. And that has worked for me like a charm.

I remember lots of flashing red lights and then lying on a bed and hearing my mom crying, I dreamed about this for a very long time. In my dream she was saying "my finger, my finger," but it wasn't her finger. She was actually saying, "My baby's finger, my baby's finger."

I remember feeling something running down my face, but

in my dream I actually saw the blood running down my face. I did get some stitches in my face and because my finger had almost been ripped off they had to sew part of my finger back on. Because I was very young I don't remember every part of that horrible day but the evidence is presented to me every time I look at my right hand.

There were five on my right hand. The enemy must have known that something good was going to come out of this right hand. The first attack was the ripping of my finger in the car, and the second came when I was about six.

I was playing with the stove, and Mom told me not to, but I went back and played with it again because it just looked pretty every time the burner got hot. It was electric burners and the red was so appealing to me. Mom came over and said, "You want to play with the stove? You think it's a joke to play with stoves? I am going to teach you a lesson."

She pulled my right hand and snatched me toward the stove as my body twisted all around. I tried pulling back, but she still had a tight grip on my little fingers until she got me close enough to the stove to press my fingers on the burner. I remember her saying now "do it again and see what happens" It may have been two fingers, but the pain was indescribable. I remember screaming and crying so badly from my soul. I don't remember any consoling or hugging after that episode all I remember after that were the blisters from the burn that hurt so bad, I could barely stand it. Mom really hurt me that day and I often looked at the hand and wondered what was going through her head to do such a thing to me. Later on I noticed that the burn was right next to the finger that was nearly ripped off.

The next attack came when I was 13. My friend Sheila, my brother Jay and I were at home while Mom and Dad were out. We went into the kitchen and there was some pie. I may have given Sheila a small piece but not a big enough for one to notice. It wasn't like she ate the whole pie, honestly it was very tiny piece, I'm not sure but someone else may have taken some that I didn't know about. When my parents got home, I began to hear my mother in the kitchen yelling, "Who ate my pie?"

She called me in off of the porch and it all happened so fast that all I remember is her screaming about the pie with a plate in her hand. I then heard a loud scream and it came from my brother Jay. My father had gone out on the front porch and kicked him in the back with his pointy shoes. I could tell that he was really hurt by the way his back was caved in and the way he was crying. I turned to tell my mother what had happened, but before I could respond, I saw a plate flying though the air. I looked down and saw the plate broken in pieces on the floor. Suddenly I felt a burning, stinging, hurting sensation that sent me into a running scream from the pit of my soul. My right index finger was split open to where you could see the bone. I couldn't believe my mother had thrown a plate at me.

When Mom threw the plate, her live-in boyfriend was on the steps listening as he always did. I ran past him with my hand full of blood and he was laughing so hard, it was like he was watching "The Last Comic Standing" or something. As I cried and screamed, he walked up the other set of stairs with his hand over his mouth, pointing at me and laughing. I was so mad at him. He made me hate him even more than I already did.

I ran to the bathroom to run water on my hand and that was the first time in my life that I had ever seen white meat or a bone. I was scared and shocked at the same time. My hand bled for a long time. I thought my mother would come to see the damage that she had done, but instead she hollered from down in the kitchen, "And if you go to the hospital you better not tell them what happened. You better make something up." At the moment, I couldn't even think to make something up. I didn't want to make something up, so instead of going to the hospital, I took care of my own cut every day until it healed itself. That was a very sad day for me and my brother. It hurt my heart to know that my bone was exposed and my mom didn't care enough to see about me, at the time I just couldn't understand why I was hated so much. What had I ever done to be treated so badly? Every once in a while I look at the scar on my hand and think to myself I have come through some rough times.

The next attack came from my ex-husband. One day I came

home from church and all of his friends were hanging out at my house as usual. I ask him to please make them leave because all I really wanted to do was come home from church and sit on my own couch without ten guys there all the time. He told me no.

When I ask him again, he told me to go upstairs. Normally I would have, but this time I wasn't going to just let those guys take over my house with all of their beer bottles all over the floor. No, not this time! I told him if he wouldn't ask them to leave, I would. Well, what did I say that for? He and I got into an argument. I had asked him nicely but firmly for them to leave. I just wanted a change to be made, but it wasn't what he wanted. We went out on the front porch to try to resolve it. He was an angry person anyway, but he was so mad at me that when he stepped out of the door, I followed him I can't remember what it was, but I copied what he said in a little voice.

He went down to the front of our gate and found the biggest rock that he could find. I had my back turned, not knowing what he was about to do. I turned around and saw a rock leaving his hand and coming toward me, I threw up my arm to block my face and the rock hit me in my right arm and in my fingers. I started bleeding and crying probably about the same time. He came running, saying, "See what you made me do? You see this?" He cursed at me and called me the word that's used for a female dog. He then came in and told all of his friends to get the F.. out and told me to get in the house. My kids were there and experienced seeing me cry and him hollering at me like I was a child. I became more afraid of him after that point. Later that night he told me he didn't remember throwing the rock; he said he blacked out. That was scary! My advice for anyone experiencing any of this is to get out as soon as you can. It never gets any better, I eventually got out but it never got better it only got worse. No matter how many tears or promises it never changed.

The next event involving my fingers happened when I was 16 and in a Job Corps building maintenance class working on bricks. I had a chisel in one hand and a hammer in the other, and I was just about to plow into the brick for the first time, all excited. I hit the chisel with the hammer and the chisel broke off into lots of pieces and scattered into all of my fingers. The same index finger that was cut with a plate, burned by the stove, and hit with a rock went into surgery to get the metal out of it. They had to go down and scrape the bone to make sure that there was no metal left inside my finger.

The Fights

It would be about 3:00 in the morning, and we would hear Dad come in the front door, drunk and cursing our mother. Then we would hear something breaking and Mom hollering and Dad yelling, "Shut the —— up!" (You can fill in the blanks). My brother and sisters and I would be lined up on the step watching those two go at it until the police showed up at the door asking them to keep it quiet. Every once in a while the police would take Dad out and he would return in the morning like nothing had happened. Between the beatings and the noise and the loud bangs, I would jump at everything.

At that time I never liked either of my parents. They made life very miserable for us youngsters. They fought, screamed and beat me all the time, and I just didn't want to live there anymore. When I was fourteen I went to live at a place called Family of Woodstock after another terrible beating. When I came home for a visit my mom and dad came out of the bedroom and he stood there with his arm around her, saying, "Tell her, Ruthie. Tell her how much we hate her. Tell her how much we wish she wasn't born. Tell her, Ruthie, how we were just talking about it in the room." Mom stood there and never said a word. She just looked at me because she never expected him to tell. I know that she felt bad because I saw just a little bit of it in her face.

Another time my father came into the house saying he owed me a whipping. He told me to lay across the bed with my pants down. I was crying already and I tried to cry just a little louder so mom could hear me and not let him beat me long. He began the beating and I cried and jumped around the bed, but this time it was different. He just started hitting me anywhere. It was like he was out for revenge on someone. I started screaming, louder and louder. I know that my mother heard me, but the screaming never moved her. The beating just continued on and on until I couldn't cry or scream anymore and all she could hear was me getting hit, then dead silence, then another hit and more dead silence.

Finally my mother came up stairs and said, "What are you trying to do to her, Raymond, kill her?" He stopped and leaned on the wall. It took him a moment. He had to pull himself together because he was out of breath. Then they both went downstairs and I lay still until the very next day.

I also remember dad hitting me in the knees with a solid rod or a stick so badly that I had to crawl down the outside steps just to try to get away from him, I couldn't walk. I got beat at school by the principal at least three times a month for acting out the abuse that I suffered at home, and then I would come home and get another beating on top of the beatings that I received on a regular basis.

This is crazy, but I would be washing dishes and my parents would come up from behind and slap me dead in the face and say, "These dishes are not clean." Or mom would call my dad, and say, "Raymond, Missy dropped silverware behind the washing machine," which was true because there were so many. Dad would come down about ten minutes later and sneak up on me and hit me straight across my back with the switch. Getting hit like that from behind actually paralyzed me in a sense of not allowing anyone to approach me from behind, or hitting me on the back even in a friendly gesture.

There was one time that mom felt really bad for me. My father had taken a long switch from off the tree and he had beaten me with it. In the process, he hit me directly across my face so that my eye was swollen and my nose and lip were busted. I was supposed to go to school the next morning but Mom let me stay home. She took me for a walk with her that day and she held my hand. I never remembered Mom ever really holding my hand in love like that. As we walked I could see the hurt in her face as she looked at my face and I could see that she wished that it had never happened to me. I can't explain it, but I looked at her and she looked at me and I saw pain for me in her face for the very first time. I guess it's not that she didn't have a heart; she just didn't have the courage or the strength to stand up for me.

I grew up being nervous all the time. I was beaten so much that I still have welts in between my legs from the switches that they chose for me and scars from the vein that got busted in my left leg. I have been through a lot. I won't tell it all, but it affected me so much that if anyone raised a hand to say "hi" to me or someone around me, I would duck. I was full of fear. For a long time I was very jumpy and scared.

I still carry some baggage as a result. I don't like it when someone comes up to me from behind and hits me on the back. I hate that with a passion. I sometimes don't like loud, playful noises when adults goof off and play fight. I start hollering, "Cut it out." It's not so bad now, but sometimes it still bothers me.

After a while I picked up a bad spirit and was filled with rage. I was so angry that when I got into fights, I couldn't bring myself to stop.

Once in the eighth grade, I was sitting at the table in the library doing schoolwork with another young lady. It was quiet until a boy came over and started messing with her. She kept telling him to leave her alone, but he wouldn't stop. I told him to leave her alone and to stop making noise because he was disturbing us. He told me to mind my business. I told him if he didn't leave our table that there was going to be trouble.

At that time, I was trying to do well in school because I had already been in numerous fights that landed me at home for five days suspension. So instead of flipping out, I walked up to the front of the library to ask the librarian to have this kid moved from our table. But he was just as cocky as I was, and he followed me to the front talking junk, like he wanted to fight. The librarian was in the back room. I tried to wait for her to come to the front, but the boy just kept talking in my ear. We got into a small argument and one thing led to another and before I knew it, the boy had kicked me in the leg.

I never liked to argue because my lips would get very tight and no words would come out, and by then I would be ready to fight.

There was no more need to talk. I felt a jolt go through my body when he kicked me. That's all it took. I turned to him and punched him dead in his face and grabbed his head and began slamming it into the library counter. Then I slammed him to the floor and placed one hand around his neck and with my right hand started beating him in the face. I felt the rage take over.

I could hear the librarian hollering at me to get off of him. I felt her trying to push me off and kicking me. I kept my left hand on the boy's neck and took my right hand and pushed the librarian so hard that she fell into the counter. I heard her yell, "Go get Mr. Bunker! Go get Mr. Bunker!" I didn't mean to push her, but I didn't like other people touching me when I was fighting because for some crazy reason, I would turn on them, too.

Anyway, I went back to beating the guy in his face and I had a lock on him that would not come loose. I saw the men come running into the room to try to break up the fight. They tried to pull me off the boy, but for some reason I could not let go of his neck. It was like my hand was locked. I saw his eyes rolling up in his head and the foam coming out of his mouth, but I just couldn't stop hitting him. Something inside of me wanted to let go. I tried and tried, and from the pit of my stomach I screamed, "Help me, God, help me." When I did that, the lock of my hand released him. When I got up off of the boy, I watched him grab his neck, choking and gasping for air. When I turned around, there were five guys standing there ready to grab me, but I screamed, "Don't touch me!"

I always screamed from the pit of my belly after a fight. It was like something in me was trying to get out. I felt like I was possessed with rage. I just kept hoping that I would never kill anyone in one of those fights, because it was so bad that once I actually thought about how I was going to kill two people who jumped me with their friends. I hadn't realized that I needed to watch my back. I always fought head up.

One time, a guy grabbed me from behind and pushed me out the door and into the snow. At first I thought he was just playing, but I soon realized that wasn't the case. The guy held me face down while the girls with him stuffed snow in my face and mouth. I kid you not; I actually saw black spots before me. I couldn't function. I felt the guy's knee in my back and one of the girls leaning on my shoulder and another helping to push my head into the snow.

I don't know how I got up, but when I did, I knew I needed to get somewhere to catch my breath and pull myself together. I ran to my counselor's office. She asked me what was wrong. I thought I was having an asthma attack or something because it took me a while to breathe properly. By the time I came back to my senses, eight security guards had already arrived. I tried to tell my counselor what had happened, but before I could get it out, the girls who had attacked me were at the dormitory doors, trying to get in to where I was.

I knew if I had not been jumped from behind, they would not have gotten the best of me, and something inside of me snapped. I saw blood. I literally saw how I was going to kill those two girls. I charged towards the door and the guards grabbed me and held me down. I screamed and kicked and hollered and fought until I couldn't struggle anymore. When I realized that they were not letting me up or out, I just cried like a big baby for over an hour. On one hand, I felt defeated, but on the other hand, I was glad that they had not let me out, because I would be in prison right now for the murders of those girls. I won't even tell you the vision in my head of how I would murder them.

They kept the door closed and no one left for at least a couple of hours. They all talked to me as much as they could, telling me that if I got into one more fight, I would be kicked out of the Job Corps program. They said that the guy and the girls would be punished for their actions, but it was up to me what I was going to do when I left the office.

They were all very nice and took a lot of time with me that day, which rarely ever happened. I was a troubled kid with no real hope in life. They must have seen that in me and that's why they wouldn't let me go. When I left the office, I went straight out to find the guy that grabbed me. I saw him and picked up one of those old metal mop buckets tops, the part that you squeeze the mop with. I began to run toward him with it to hit him in the head, but he saw me coming and ran. As I chased him, he said, "I'm sorry.

They told me that they were just playing. They told me to grab you and bring you outside because they wanted to play a game on you. I swear, I didn't know."

I dropped the bucket top and grabbed him up by his shirt, balling up my fist. He kept saying he really didn't know. I looked at him for a moment, then I let him up from the bench and walked away. I knew once again that I needed to get my act together. Even though all the hatred and anger stemmed from the birth of negativity from my parents, it was still my duty to try to do what was right. I knew that I had to talk to God about this one. It seemed as if there was nothing or no one that could help me out of my trauma, I was at the end of my rope. The pain was so bad that I couldn't take it anymore. I always wondered about my life and what would become of me. I always wanted better for my life and I always put forth for good to happen in my but it always seemed as evil was always present in my life. One day I called on the name of Jesus and something real miraculous happened. I didn't know Jesus like others knew him. I just knew that when I put my bible on my body he healed me without me even knowing his name. I ask him to help me. I wasn't raised in a home of Christ, or gospel music or anything that even looked like Jesus but something happened when I called on his name. Something real, something tangible began to happen to me. When I called him he answered me. God's love came in and he filled me and replaced that anger with love, because that's all I ever wanted anyway. And that's how I was able to forgive my parents and love them with an unconditional love. It was like a "until death do us part" kind of thing. I never thought that I could trade my hate for love, but I am full of love. I couldn't understand how I could love these two people who made my life miserable and treated me so unjustly. And then God turned around and used me as an example to love the one who hurt me the most. Wow, it really blew my mind.

To be honest with you, after God came in and healed me, I didn't look at either one of them in that negative way again. We all became the very best of friends. I remember it clear as day. I was sixteen. Once again my father was in jail and I was in another fight. It seemed all hope was gone for me. I went to God on my knees and I told Him, "If you help me to forgive my parents, I will serve you." I knew things had to change and I needed to see a difference.

Well, lo and behold, that same year my dad came out of jail and never touched another drink, and soon after that my mom gave her life to Christ, and we all began a new life. Now everything wasn't hunky-dory right away. Remember, to everything there is a season and all must go through a process. But God began to do it and I saw the change little by little over time. God is good, all we have to do is trust him and believe that all things are possible and he will do it.

Angels Watching Over Me

I was 14 years of age when I began praying because I had asthma really bad. I didn't know much about it, but I did notice that when I prayed, I would get better immediately. So I decided that every time that I would leave the house, I would pray, I didn't understand why I would pray at that time but there was just something inside that told me to do it.

One night it was very late when my mom sent me out to get her a pack of cigarettes, which she often did even though it could be midnight or later. That night my friend Serena and I were on our way to the store and I said to her, "Let's pray. We should never leave the house without praying." We prayed at the bottom of the hill, we then began to walk and as we almost reached the top, a white jeep pulled up beside of us and a voice said, "You two look like the two guys that just robbed the convenience store."

We both were wearing sweat jackets with hoods, so we pulled the hoods off and I replied, "We are not guys! We are girls, and I am on my way to the store for my mother to get her cigarettes." The man said to get in the car, but we didn't get in. His voice began to rise and he said, "Get in the car now!" I said no. He reached over and pulled out a gun and said, "Get in!"

All of a sudden out of nowhere—and I mean literally nowhere—cops swarmed the top of the corner. There were about six to eight cop cars and they were chasing somebody. The guy who had pulled the gun on us dropped it and took off. He went to the top of the hill and made a left and I never saw him again. Being scared out of my wits, I ran to the top of the hill. Since I didn't want to be accused of stealing anything that I didn't steal, I went straight to one of the officers who was standing there and ask him, "Did anyone rob the convenience store and were they looking for two guys?" He said no, and I told him what had just happened, including that the guy had pulled a gun on us. They put in a call to the dispatcher and went looking for him. I don't know if they ever got him, but I am surely glad that we prayed because if we hadn't, maybe today I would be a statistic.

My photo might be on a milk carton with the words, "Have you seen this child?" Oh, I truly thank God for prayer!

Bad Habits

I had a very bad habit of stealing. Sometimes I felt like I had to steal; other times I did it just because I wanted to. I remember being excited about going on a school trips, but the only thing that I had for lunch would be a peanut butter sandwich. I would get up and make my sandwich early in the morning and on my way to school I would look in a trashcan for a brown paper bag or a small plastic one. I wanted to look like I had just as much food as the others had. Little did they know what was really inside of my lunch bag. I would be so hungry that I would wait for the other children to get off of the bus and then take as much food as I could out of their bags and stuff it in my little bag, eating the rest as fast as I could.

In the third grade, there was a little girl by the name of Sandy who always had the best snacks in class. I would stare at her while she ate because her food looked so good. One day I got up the nerve to ask if she would give me a piece of her chocolate cake because she always had 2 ring dings. She gave me a nasty look and rolled her eyes and said no. I thought to myself that she didn't have to say it like that. So one day when she got up to go to the bathroom, I went over into her desk and took the whole snack and stuffed it in my mouth before she got back. Later on when it was snack time, I was over by one of the other children and I watched her go into her desk and pull out her empty bag. She had a look of shock on her face and began to cry. I felt bad watching her cry but I was really hungry and at that time I was really just in survival mode even though I kept stealing food every chance I got.

As I got older, my friend Sheila and I would go into a store called Woolworth's where we would walk in and take off our old shoes and put on a new pair right in the store. Sheila and I had a new pair of sneakers every other week along with anything else that we could find in the store. My habit grew to where I would go to the elderly and offer to take out their trash and when they turned their back, I would steal some money out of their purse. I am not proud to say that, but it was a part of my life. Nobody had to tell me that it was wrong. I knew it was wrong, but I did it anyway. It's not that I couldn't help myself; it was just a bad habit that I wasn't willing to change at that time. Every time I stole money I went and bought food.

Sometimes Sheila, my friend Serena, and I would want to go roller skating but since we had no money, I would steal for all of us. We would walk to the roller skating rink with no coat and leave with new coats from the coat racks, along with a few pocketbooks with some money in them. Sometimes we would even get lucky and find a pair of someone's skates and take them too, and ride all the way home, with a stop at the store to get some snacks.

By the time I was sixteen, I had become very careless about stealing. My sister and I would go to the grocery store with the permission of my mother to go and steal some food for the house.

We went into a store called Grand Union as much as we could and steal steaks, pork chops, and any other kind of meat that we could get our hands on-until one day we got caught. We made our way through the register and paid for three loaves of bread that was our way of covering up the things that we stole. We always bought something to make it look like we were really shopping.

On our way out the door we heard a voice say, "Hey, you. Stop right there." I kept walking like I didn't hear them until they came up behind us and grabbed our shoulders.

They took us in the back of the store and the store manager said, "Give me all of my stuff back now." They looked in my sister's baby bag and took all the meat out.

Then they searched my bag and one of them said, "Oh yeah, and get the deck of cards out of her back pocket." I just knew that we were going to play some spades when we got home that night.

The manager started hollering at me, saying, "Do you know who you are stealing from? Do you know...?"

I said, "Who?"

He said, "Me. I am the manager of this store."

Me, being wise, said, "So I don't care whose store this is."

He got mad at me and said, "Call the cops. They're going to jail."

I said, "I don't care about any jail. Call the cops."

My sister was sitting there five months pregnant, not saying a word. I began to curse at the man. I told him I would steal his things again. It got real nasty in the store with my mouth. Finally two cops came. They had the same last name, Schatzel and Schatzel. I told them I wanted to go to jail, Arrest me. I don't know why I was so hostile, but I was mad.

The officers put cuffs on both of us and placed us in the car.

While we were riding, the officers said to me, "So you want to go to jail?"

I said, "Yeah, I think I will like it there" and I asked, "Do they have a TV?"

They said yes and I said, "Good. That's all I need."

They talked nice to us and treated us very well, and the ride wasn't that bad. We were taken inside and fingerprinted. Of course I had to go on trying to be big and bad, and I told the lady, "Don't twist my fingers like that. What's wrong with you?" She and I got into an argument and she took my fingers and twisted them even harder. Then she told me if I didn't calm down that I would be in solitary confinement starting right then. I came to my senses real quick. We were in jail for four days, and nobody came to see us.

No one bailed us out either, and our bail was only $100.

I began to figure out right then and there that I had to start really looking out for myself. My boyfriend at the time didn't even come to get me out, and maybe that was because he was to busy having an affair with another girl who actually was my cousin. My sister and I sat in that jail and we both realized that jail was not a place that either of us wanted to be. When we were brought out, we were shackled at our hands and feet. It was so humiliating to have to walk out in front of people with cuffs on. I was praying that we were going to be released, because I did not want to go back in there again.

I also felt very bad for my sister because she was pregnant. She was usually just as mouthy as I was, but not that time. I guess I had said enough for the both of us. When it was my turn to go in front of the judge, my whole attitude had changed-no more cursing or trying to be a Miss Know-it-all. I was very humble when he asked if I had learned my lesson.

"Yes, sir. I certainly did," I told him.

"Okay, I am going to release you today, but if I see you in my courtroom within the next six months, you will be doing thirty days in jail," he warned me.

"I promise you will never see me again," I told him.

My sister and I were released the same day but at separate times. I remember walking home, looking up at the sky, and being aware of how beautiful the day was. The sun was shining, and the grass had never looked greener. I made up in my mind that day that I was going to try to do better. I started by going home and taking a long hot shower and then I went back to the Grand Union, found the manager of the store that I was banned from, and apologized sincerely to him. I told him that he didn't have to let me back in the store to shop. I just wanted to come in to tell him how bad I felt and that I was turning over a new leaf.

He told me because I apologized with such sincerity that I was allowed back in the store. From that time on, every time I went into the store I acknowledged him and let him know that I was still doing very well. When I saw the officers who had arrested us, I told them that jail had done wonders for me and that I was a changed young lady. From that time on, the cops and I became very good friends. They checked up on me through the years to see how I was doing. And I am proud to report that from that time on, I never stole anything ever again.

I learned another lesson from stealing: because I stole some things in life, lots of things were stolen from me. I stole $97 from a little old lady and when she found out that it was me, I had to return the money-well, what was left of it. To my surprise, when I grew up, I had put money under my mattress and I left a babysitter in my house. When I got home, I needed the money and it was gone. I looked all through the house, and finally came to the conclusion that the babysitter had taken it. I walked down to her house and her father answered the door. I told him that I believed that his daughter had just stolen $100 from under my bed. He asked her and she said she hadn't taken it.

I left her house very angry. I couldn't help but think about when I stole that lady's money and now it was my turn to be stolen from.

I went home and within twenty minutes there was a knock at my door. It was the babysitter and her father. He said, "I just want to apologize to you. My daughter did take your money." He made her give me what she had and he assured me that he would make her pay back the rest of it. It was almost as though I was reliving what that old lady must have gone through.

I have learned some valuable lessons in life. I have done a few things in my life that have come back to get me, but the good thing is that all of that is over. I have paid my debt to God for all of my wrong doings. Even though there were some small things, it all feels the same when you are getting what you deserve. I realized that if you sow good things, even if bad things come, know for sure that good is on its way and if you sow badly, just know that bad is on its way to get you, too. I am a living witness that as sure as you dish it out, it will be served right back at you-but when it reaches you, it will be on a platter.

My Face in the Toilet Bowl

You think I didn't want to die or commit suicide. Yes, I did. I remember being at the end of my rope. I'd had enough of everything. I felt as if I couldn't handle any more. I went into the bathroom, put my face over the toilet bowl, and I began to pray to God. I said, "God I hate my life and I don't want to live anymore." As I said this prayer, my face began to go deeper into the toilet bowl until I could feel the water from the toilet in my face; but, at this point, I didn't care. I had lost all sense of self. As I lay there, I said a little prayer. I said, "God, today I am going to kill myself." I spoke to God with my inside voice because I didn't have enough strength to say it out loud. I said, "If you want me to live then you are going to have to show me that you want me here. If not, today is my last day here on earth." I said, "I have $1.00 in my pocket and my phone bill is $21.00. If you want me to live, you have to have someone give me $20.00 without me asking. If you do this without me asking anyone then I know that you want me to live and I won't kill myself today." I pulled myself up from that toilet bowl and proceeded with my day. I caught a ride to my doctor's appointment. When the visit was over, my 4 year old daughter and I began to walk down the street. As I walked up near a driveway, a lady pulled out. It startled me because although she was in her car, we met face to face. She said, "Oh hi." And I said, "Hi" back to her. She began to apologize because she didn't see me there. At the same time, I was thinking to myself that I wasn't paying attention because my mind was not thinking about anything. We began to talk and she asked me, "Do you believe in angels?" I said, "Yes." Then she said, "There is a show that is coming on tonight at 8pm. You should watch it. Here is my number. Call me and let me know how you like it." I said "Ok." Then she asked, "Would you be offended?" I responded, "By what?" Then she said, "If I give you $20.00." I stood there in shock for a moment then I took the $20.00. She then pulled off and said, "Have a good day. God bless you." I took that $20.00 from the woman I didn't know and went and paid my telephone bill. I began to cry because I knew without a shadow of a doubt that God loved me and He didn't want me to kill myself. He loved me enough to save my life that day.

Later on, after building a relationship with this beautiful woman, she told me that she was standing at her window sad because her children had just gone off to college. She prayed to God that if she had any mothering skills that she could pass on to someone in need, then please send them. Wow! God was working on both of our behalves because we both had something that we needed from Him. I couldn't believe that God could and would do that for me. Did that mean that He had a purpose for my life? Did He think that I was important enough to save? Yes, I was! Now, whenever I feel any kind of way and I go through situations, I always look back on this time in my life and say to myself, "I know that God truly loves me." I call this beautiful lady Mrs. V. She has never let me fall and has always been my saving grace. I consider her my Guardian Angel here on earth. No matter when I call, she answers me. She has been more than a friend. She has been a mother to me when I didn't understand my life and the things I had suffered. I appreciate how she has poured her knowledge into me daily and stayed on me when I thought I was going right but I was actually going wrong. She loves me and my family without cause and I could never repay her for all the time and effort she has given me. All I can say is, "Thank you, Mrs. V. for being everything that I needed in a mother here on earth. I love and appreciate you from the tippy top to the bottom part of my heart."

Q's Death

Nobody ever told me that at the age of fifteen I would watch a man being beaten to death.

One night I was just hanging out with a few friends and looking up on the third floor at all the action there. There were lots of running and something didn't seem right. I was standing about 20 feet away from my friend S.J. when all of a sudden I began to feel I was standing all alone. I felt something strange. It's almost like I had radar in my head or something detecting that something that was not right. But I still didn't move. I noticed a guy on the third floor, still not knowing what was going on.

My friend Q was standing about 10 feet in front of me. We never passed any words on that day, but he was one of the kindest guys that I had ever met. Before I could say hello to him, I felt someone running up behind me so fast that I never even had a chance to turn around. He was running with his fist in the air. Before I knew it Q was down, having been punched in the face by the runner. He didn't move because he was immediately knocked unconscious. As I watched his limp body hit the ground, I couldn't move. I believe I went into sudden shock. But the worst part was it didn't stop there. As Q lay still on the ground, this guy began kicking him. Then from out of nowhere, another guy came and grabbed Q's head and began slamming it on the ground until I heard a crack. He had cracked Q's skull. Amazingly, Q jumped straight up out of the unconscious state he had been in, and ran for what he may have thought was safety. I couldn't believe my eyes. What has this world come to?

All of a sudden I heard a loud scream from Q as he tried to get into someone's apartment. His speech was terribly slurred, but his screams were of agony. I heard someone say, "I'm going to call an ambulance." Then I heard Q speak clearly for the first time, as he screamed "No! Leave me alone." At that moment, I thought that he would be all right and pull through.

When the ambulance arrived, they went down to the apartment where he was and tried to calm him down, but his screams were becoming more and more piercing. Finally he was in the ambulance. I still stood there in shock. I was thinking this did not just happen—or did it?

After going home that night, I called the hospital and they told me that Q was in a coma. I was so hurt to know that this sort of thing could happen to people. I was traumatized. I kept reliving the incident over and over in my head. I heard the scream, the crack, the running—just over and over and over.

I kept calling day after day, but there was no real change. When I called again for what would be the last time, the hospital asked who I was and if I was family. They had never asked that before, so I began to fear the worst. What was it that they were trying to say to me? I was a little nervous, but I still wanted to know how my friend was. I said, "No, I am just a very close friend," and the pause between my last words and her voice seemed like forever. She finally said, "I'm sorry; he died a little while ago."

I put the phone down and sat back, and I cried with everything that was in me.

"No!" I screamed. "I'm going to see him again. I'll see him walking down the street smiling or I'll see him getting on the school bus in the morning with his cheerful and jolly self."

After all the tears and pain, reality set in that he was not coming back. I'd never see him again.

Nobody ever told me that years later just thinking about it that I would cry just like it was yesterday. I never understood how someone so nice, kind and had a beautiful giving soul could be killed. It was the worst year of my teenage life. Oh how my soul mourned after that happened but I didn't know that this kind of pain could affect change in other people's lives. I took the pain of Q and I turned it into something positive. I wanted to be a better person and if I could intervene to help save anyone's life I wanted to do it for the better of society. I remember one day how I was sitting in my car and a young man ran by and someone said he was going to get a gun.

As he came out of the house with the gun in his pants, My motherly instincts kicked in and I said to him, "Listen young man, before you shoot that gun, you have a choice.

Sometimes we get caught up in the moment; it's called the heat of passion. But if you just think about what you are about to do, you can save someone else's life. What if you hit an innocent bystander?

It's not fair. Think about what you are about to do before you do it. It's really not worth it."

He needed me to intervene at that moment. The look that he had in his eyes when he ran through to get the gun was quite scary, but he needed a quick reality check. Well, low and behold, thank god, he never shot the gun. He came back and told me that he thought about what I said. Man that did my heart so good that all I could do is thank god and think about a life being saved. Maybe I couldn't help Q, but I am helping others to think twice before they make a mistake that they will regret later.

So rest in peace, Q, and just know that your memory lives on in my heart, that I might change the way the world thinks when it comes to violent acts. I love you, Q, always. Thanks for being so nice to me.

Fear Had Gripped Me for a Long Time

I will share all of my fears with you. These are things that have actually gone through my mind. "Will something bad happen to me? Will he leave me? Will he cheat on me? Close the bathroom door, something could be staring at me. I can't sleep at night unless someone is there with me (after the rape). Am I pretty enough? Wasn't I light enough (because Grandma wanted Dad with a light-skinned woman, but Mom was black)? Will my life ever be worth living? Will he still love me if I take my weave out (because Mom told me at 9 that my scalp was dead, so I believed her)? Why would he stay with me; what is so special about me?" But then one day I said to myself, "I am loveable. Nothing is going to happen to me unless God says so. If He leaves me then He wasn't for me. Nothing is staring at me from the bathroom darkness because I just checked the room and it was empty. I don't need to be light-skinned to be pretty; pretty runs in my blood, through my heart, and out of my skin. I am beautiful. I don't need a weave, but I choose to wear one. I do have nice hair up under it. No, Mommy, my scalp wasn't dead; I just didn't know that I had lupus until I was grown. Why would a man stay with me? My question back to myself was, 'Why wouldn't he stay with me?' I am not only a good woman, I am a great woman.

Outlet

I had an outlet throughout all my misery. Her name was Joan Perpetua. She was a saint if I knew one. A mother of three girls, she had a beautiful house with a pool in the yard, her house was always clean, and she cooked the best food. We all ate at one table and she let me eat as much as I wanted. She was a very giving person.

She allowed me into her home—and a home it was! I went down every day as much as Mom would allow. Her girls had nice rooms with bunk beds. I always liked the top. When I went to her house, I realized that I wanted to become a good mother, I wanted a nice clean house and I wanted a family that functioned properly. I had always wanted a nice back yard.

She made me want to become a complete woman. Every time I left my dysfunctional home to go to her house, I felt the difference. No one at her house was cursed, beaten, or mistreated. No one got in trouble for going into the fridge for a snack, and the girls always hugged and loved their mom. Even though she was a single mom, she carried the house with lots of love and control. She even had enough love for me. There was no love lacking at all

I was a handful yes I was I had a bad mouth. I was always hyper and hungry, but she never threw me away. I came from a house of beatings, lots of alcohol, betrayal and everything out of order. At Beth Anne's house everything was always the same. It always had structure, love, peace, girl fights, making-up, hugs, and food. It was always clean and for the first time I saw a dishwasher. In my house I was the automatic dishwasher. It was nice to finally put something else to good use besides me.

I have seen Joan upset, but she was still calm to me. Even when she had to raise her voice, it never felt like a threat, I could still feel the love because of her example; I have raised three beautiful young ladies alone. I learned that I didn't have to beat their brains out to get a point across. I didn't have to punch or kick them to get their attention. When I became a single mother I knew I could do it alone and still have a well-functioning home. I don't think that she knows this but she taught me how to love and to properly chastise my children, how to work hard, and then come home to cook and care for my family the right way. I will never be able to thank her enough for giving of herself and just doing what came naturally to this beautiful Italian woman. Yes, she was so pretty. I could never imagine someone so beautiful staying alone for so long. I couldn't understand it as a child, but she helped me by her example to stay alone for almost seven years later. Joan is a woman that I've always had a great appreciation for. I love her because she cared enough to share.

How I Met Joan

I was in school minding my own little business and there was a new girl in my fourth grade class that I had never seen before.

A boy began picking on her, and I never liked people messing with the new people or the underdogs of the class. I was all for them. She wasn't bothering or saying anything to anyone, but this boy continued to harass her. I told him to leave her alone, but he continued his reign of terror and she started to cry. Since he wouldn't listen, I got up from my seat and went over to him and we got into a fight. Needless to say, I kicked his butt. After being sent to the office, I was allowed to come back to class. I walked over to her and said, "Hi, my name is Michelle." She told me her name was Beth. I promised to protect her. That very day I walked her home and we told her mom what had happened. I told her mother that I would walk her home every day because of the mean kids at school.

As time progressed, I began teaching her how to fight. I would rough her up a little bit and she would cry. I told her to stop crying, that I wanted her to be able to stand on her own two feet. It didn't take long before Beth Anne was feisty and ready to take on anyone who tried her. I didn't have to protect her anymore.

In junior high school, we began going our own separate ways, but no matter where I go in life I will always have that special bond in my heart for the whole Perpetua family. They took me in and treated me like I was one of the family. Even though our meetings since then have been few and far between, when I see Cindy, we always talk just as though I have just met up with my long lost sister. We stop on the sidewalk, in the stores, or wherever, and it's always a good conversation. and it's always a pleasure. Chris has grown up to become a wonderful person. I don't get to see her as much, but when I do I always tell her I love her and how beautiful she is.

I love the Perpetua family: You will always be in my heart forever. Thanks for the love.

Joan, Can I Tell You This?

You didn't know how wounded
I was when I came to you or
Maybe deep inside you did
But the love that all of you
Showed me began the healing process for me
See, at the time I didn't know that real love
existed
I didn't know what acceptance was
But you took me in and treated me better than
I expected

I will never be able to thank you all enough
For loving me through all of my hardships
For because of you, I now stand stronger and
taller
Than I have ever been
For because of you I can love my children
Into their purpose and their destiny
For because of you and your unselfish love
I am a whole woman
Because you allowed me to see into your life
You showed me what it would be like to
Live my life with hope, dreams and fulfillment
Thank you my love of a mother that I needed
Thank you for the love of a sister that I wanted
Thank you for opening your doors to a child
With no vision
Thank you for the hope that lay within you
Thank you for the hope that lay within you

Chapter 5

Filled with the Holy Spirit

I faithfully gave my life to Christ at about the age of seventeen. I needed to be delivered from smoking cigarettes. I had picked up the bad habit when Mom and Dad left their cigarette packs lying around the house. Sheila and I would sneak and puff as much as we could. It was a fun game at first—until we became addicted.

After a while neither one of us could stop. We both started smoking at fourteen. After about three years of it, I began to feel its affects.

I couldn't breathe properly, I couldn't run as fast, and it made my breath stink.

I really wanted to be a true Christian and I knew that I didn't want to smoke while teaching God's word. I would take a puff of the cigarette and say, "Satan, I rebuke you in the name of Jesus," then I would take another puff and I would repeat myself. I knew there was power in the name of Jesus. I know it sounds funny, but I put my trust in God to deliver me from the addiction of a pack and a half of cigarettes a day. My nerves were bad and it calmed me down every time I smoked, and you know what? God came through and he delivered me to where I never had to smoke again.

My last cigarette was when I was seventeen.

God knows all things and he knew the ministry that I was to do for him would not allow me to smoke. He had set a mission for my life. I went on and ask God to fill me with his precious Holy Spirit. It didn't happen right away, but that didn't stop me from seeking and asking him to fill me. Finally about a year and a half later, I was lying in my bed in the middle of the night and I heard God's voice say, "Get up and go and get a white sheet and lie on the couch downstairs."

I began to try to negotiate with God; I told him that I was tired, and asked if I could do it tomorrow. He said the same words again, and I said, "I can't, God. Savanna is nursing right now."

Now the funny thing is that she was sleeping and just hadn't released from nursing. I was trying to tell God, I couldn't move, because if I did, Savanna would wake up. As soon as I said that, I heard a loud pop and Savanna released off of my breast. I told God, "OK, I will move now; I get the point." I felt the spirit leading me as if someone held my hand the whole way down stairs.

As I lay down on the couch, I said, "God, I have never done this before, I don't know what to say or do. I will just begin to worship you, OK?" I began saying softly, "Thank you, Jesus. God, I love you. God, you are so worthy." I did this for about five minutes and out of the clear blue, I felt a force of power come into my feet and move up through the bottom of my legs. As soon as it hit my knees, I shouted, "No, Lord, no!" It was so powerful that it scared me. At that very moment, I felt the power starting to move slowly back down my legs and go back out through my feet, that let me know right there that God is a gentlemen and he will never force himself on you.

As I felt him moving out I got excited and said, "God, please don't go! Please come back! I was afraid. I didn't know what to expect. Please, God, please don't go, please come back," and as I lay there, the power came again, just as strong as it had been the first time. Not afraid anymore, this time I allowed God to do his job. His presence went all through my feet again, right back up through my legs and into my knees and up into my inner being all the way up through my body, right up to my head and back out through my mouth. When I open my eyes from being with God all night, I was still speaking in a heavenly language, It was the best feeling that I have ever experienced.

I got up and knew in my heart that I had been changed. Right there is where I believe God placed love in my heart and took away the hate, because that's where I felt everything spiritual began for me. I can't explain it, but that's where I began having dreams and open visions. I had an open vision as a child, but that was the only experience I remember. Now I was seeing things much more clearly. God was showing me awesome things that people just would not believe if I told them. My dreams became so real that I would tell people about it, and within a few days the dream would happen. I had to be really careful with my gift.

The gift had gotten so real that when I heard about a nine year- old little girl with cancer, I felt sad for her and I told her mom that I would pray for her. I just reached down and touched her shoulder, and when I did that, I felt the curse that had passed down to her by someone in her family. I said, "God, it's not her fault. Please, God, release this curse from this child's life and please, God, allow her to live."

I let the little girl go along with her mother, and when I saw the mom about a month later, she told me that her daughter had gone into remission. I felt so good because I knew that the curse had been broken off of her life. When I saw her again nine years later, she told me that her daughter was 18 and still in remission. It did my heart wonders to know that God can give you a power like that to help His wounded souls.

My nephew had warts all over his hand, at least ten of them and a new little baby one coming on his pinky finger. His mother asked me to pray for him. I did so and within two days, he woke up and there was not one wart left on his fingers, not even the new one growing on his pinky finger. Before I prayed for him, she had told me that they wanted to do minor surgery to cut off the warts.

I said, "No, we have more power in healing if we just believe that God is going to do it." The same thing happened to his little brother who had two warts. We prayed those away, too.

God's power stayed with me, and then I started going through rough times with the relationship and the enemy began trying to play with my mind and make me feel depressed. I know that I had God on my side, but I looked at my situation and not God. I continued to walk by faith and not by sight for a while and it was great, but when the ex started cheating on me, I took my focus off of God. I felt God had let me down, when in reality it was the person that I chosen to be in my life with me. He wasn't saved; he couldn't get me to my next level; he couldn't even get me to my next month's rent. He was not the one that God chose for me, so I had to suffer the consequences of an unequally-yoked relationship that God tells us to avoid anyway.

I was so messed up; I went from church to the clubs.

What, me a church girl in the clubs? Yes, it was a little uncomfortable for a while because I was never a club kind of girl. First I was abused, then I became a mother—and that was my life. I felt it was time to see what was really out there. For a while I had lots of fun, but at night my conscience would haunt me because I knew that God was calling me back to help the many people out there who were hurting and needed me. I kept running not only to get over the cheating part, but now he was trying to kill me. It seemed like one thing after another.

Now that I was out in the world, it felt like I had slapped God right in the face because I picked up another unsaved man and began to live with him. What in the world was I thinking? God was trying to help me, and I was running right back into the hands of the enemy. Of course we were having intercourse, and that was killing me on the inside because the more that you give of your body without being married, the more you end up giving over a part of your soul, since you have intertwined your souls into one. What he is, you are, and what you are, he is.

Somehow we get all caught up when the man comes over the next day telling you sweet nothings and how he dreamed about you and how he just can't seem to get you off of his mind or out of his system. He wears on you, and you, being dumb—or anyway I was being dumb—just give in. We fall head over heels, first giving some of our time, then giving of our feelings, then giving some of our space, then our hugs and kisses, and finally our sex. The worst part is that when we give our sex, we are actually giving our love, and when we give our love, we are giving it to someone who doesn't even know the concept of love. If he or she did, we would have never crossed the line together.

When we give so much, we don't even realize that we just gave up the most important love in our lives, which is God. We put a man or a woman before God and he or she doesn't even serve God.

After putting our relationship down with God to cover our hurts, guess who it is that we have to come back to when that new man hurts us? That's right—God.

After I messed myself up, I tied the knot, and God began to show up again and show me some favor—but that wasn't until seven years later. I had been going to church and trying to do the very best that I could to serve Him with everything in me. I was still dealing with lots of nonsense, but I didn't let that stop me.

I was at a church service one night and we were all singing— my brother, my friends, and a few others. All of a sudden from out of nowhere I felt a power hit me in my stomach and travel through my inner man, and a big note came out of my mouth. I couldn't believe it. Everyone around me stood still and the note just kept coming. I felt a power rumbling in my stomach. Basically what God had just done was put the Holy Spirit in my singing.

When I open my mouth, people's lives will be changed. I asked God why did he do this for me, and he answered, saying, "I gave it to you at the age of 27 because now I can trust you."

I just started rejoicing that God would bless me like that. I didn't feel that I deserved it, but He blessed me one day out of the blue.

That's why I sing the way that I do. He gave me power and another chance to make it right. I am not going to say that I haven't made a few more mistakes along the way, but God has aligned everything together in my life now because he had to prepare me to go to a nation of people that he has for me to reach. That's awesome! So when people don't ring my phone off of the hook or they are not responding by mail when I send out my CD's, I don't take it personally. Rather, I take it that God is up to something and while he is working it out, I'll just stay busy working in the field until he calls. And one day he will call. As a matter of fact, I think I hear him calling right now. I'm just kidding. I have to continue to work for my Savior because God has a plan for all of our lives. We are not perfect, we are just forgiven. And because we are forgiven, God has allowed me to dream again, and see things again, not as much as before, but he keeps giving me glances into some things and they do come to pass. I don't put anything past God. He could show up and hit me with another one of those fireballs and there's no telling what that one will be for. I am now a focused young lady and I appreciate time that is well spent getting to know my one and only Savior, Jesus Christ.

Love

The feeling of great intent
Is so overwhelming or just plain wishful?
Is it just me or is it just the way the universe
calls us as
Humans to be
We feel with everything within us
We care from the known
But to some unknown
We are created by a great being
So what is it?
Who are we?
Where is it that we stand for love's sake?
Why it is that love is so strong
Why is it that love carries the power
Of an unseen force that thrusts you into an
eternity of thoughts
And no real understanding
Who can really say that they understand love?
Can any man pinpoint it?
We find it
And then
It takes a lifetime
To figure out what it really is
If you think that you lose love
Love is really never lost
Because we experience love everyday
We experience it when waking up
That's God saying in a subtle way, good
morning
I love you
It's your child's smile in the morning or
Their big yawn on their way to bed at night
It's the air we breathe
Or the shifting and the changing of the weather

That says yes I change all the time
But yet I still stay the same, get it
I will suffer for loves sake
And for the sake of love
I will suffer
Who can call it?
Who can even touch it?
It's beyond a feeling
From the beginning of time
To the long lasting of eternity
Will we ever know love?
Or how love will last
Who are you?
You unknown species
Where did you come from?
How is it that you can live in my soul?
How did you even enter?
Who allowed you to come in?
He says you did
Who?
How did you enter in me?
And you entered in without force
And I didn't even see you when you came in.
Where will we go?
What will we find?
Why are you here for me?
Who are you?
May I ask!!!!!
Who are you?
It's me
Who?
Me
Me who?
It's me
God!

Chapter 6

I'm Not in the Dark Anymore

I tried to cover up the hurt in my life with laughter, fighting, and even trying to find someone to love me the way that I desired to be loved. Any attention would do, even if it meant drawing a crowd to watch me fistfight. I stood alone, but for the sake of seeing my name blown up the next day for whooping some guy's butt, I put myself out there. There were many times that I was afraid, but for some strange reason I would never back down. God, I was hurting so bad, I really needed my Savior, but since I didn't have Him at that time, I believed if I could find someone to lavish my love on that he would love me too. It took three bad relationships to find out that I shouldn't chase after love, that instead I should allow love to come to me naturally. In searching I found more than I bargained for: pain, abuse, a cheater, a liar and a thief. I didn't expect all of that.

The very first relationship that I entered into was not healthy at all. I ended up with a man who secretly smoked crack. He stole everything that we owned; everything that wasn't nailed down, he sold. He stole our rent money, the VCR, the sword given me as a gift from my brother. Incredibly, he and his father even sold the food out of the refrigerator that I needed to feed my family at Christmas time.

As I wrote earlier, I was mad at God for years for allowing me to end up like this. I was trying to become an early Christian and I just didn't think that it was fair that I had to suffer with all of the Filled with the Holy Spirit negativity. Now that I have grown up and learned a lot about life, I realize that it was not God's fault, it was mine. When you marry or date a man or woman who runs out into the world and does anything that he or she is big and bad enough to do, you take on the same thing that person takes on. If he spends the money, it means you don't have any money. If he sleeps around and gets a disease, then you get the same disease that he brings home. If he stays out all night drinking and partying, then you suffer the consequence of not having your loved one at home with you.

I couldn't be mad at God. It was never His fault; it was my own doing. I allowed this man to enter my life. I saw signs early on when I caught him up the street in bed with my very own cousin, but I allowed him to woo me into believing that he loved me. I fell for it because I was naive and I wanted to be loved so badly that I let any and everything go on in my life just for the sake of love.

But that wasn't love because even during the relationship when I got pregnant, he was cheating with one of my good friend's sisters.

I went through so much that it overtook me and I had a nervous breakdown. I ended up in the hospital at the age of twenty, crying my poor little heart out over life and all it had given to me. I just knew that I was going to die. It felt awful. I literally felt my mind leave from in front of me and move over to the side and just sit there. I couldn't reach for it or nothing. Everything in front of me became black. I felt myself slipping; my insides were shaking for weeks. When I realized that my mind was on the side of me and not inside anymore, all I could say was, "God, please don't let me lose my mind." I said it over and over again. All I could do was pray that prayer.

As I felt myself slipping, I cried and balled myself up in the hospital bed, saying, "I can't stay here. I have got to get out of here." I went to the front desk and ask if I could I go home, and they told me no. I began to scream, "Please let me out. Please can I go home?" and once again they said no. They told me to wait until I had seen the doctor and he would make the decision. So I went back to my room trying to be stable and I waited and cried, waited some more and cried some more.

Finally the doctor came and asked me several questions. I tried to answer him with a straight face, and told him that I was all right now and I was ready to be released. He looked at me and said I wasn't ready.

I said, "Doctor, yes I am. Please."

He replied, "You can't be ready. You made a threat to kill

yourself and your children by driving them into a tree. You said you didn't want to leave your small children with a man like that. No, you are not ready." He got up and walked out.

Now he'd done it! I really went off then; I couldn't help myself, I was holding in all of my tears just to get through the doctor's visit. All of a sudden there came a puddle of streaming cries, an outburst from the pit of my soul. I did say those things about dying. I didn't want to hurt my children, but I thought that I loved them so much that no one would be able to love them like I did. It's true I had felt that I was going to drive into a tree after school that day. I didn't feel like I could make it home. In fact, I had the school call my sister and ask her to come and get the children for me, to take them home and to care for them. I loved them so much, I couldn't dare hurt them, but because I had the thought, it was considered just as bad as doing the act.

I knew that I needed help. The abuse I'd suffered in my life was quite overwhelming. I couldn't handle it anymore.

So I stayed in the hospital, praying for strength. I needed help but no one in the hospital could help me; this situation was too deep. It was like they were only there to do their job and that was it. All I had was the hope that Jesus would and could rescue me.

What really snapped me back into reality was that I was able to make a phone call home to my children's father. He answered and I said hello, and he said hello. I started to cry because I was hurting so bad. It was Christmas and I wasn't home. All I could remember about the house was the beautiful Christmas tree that I put up for my children with no presents under it because of this man. I proceeded with the conversation after getting my thoughts together and ask him what he was doing. He replied, "Getting high."

"What? Getting high? Why?" I asked him. "Don't you see what you are doing to our family?" He couldn't say anything for blowing on his drug, and after a moment he said, "I know."

I began to cry again. After I hung up that phone, an inner strength came to me and I said, "I am about to kill myself over you and you are getting high!"

Before I knew it I began to feel a pinch of help coming to me.

My mind was starting to become just a little bit clearer. I still felt hurt, empty, and sad, but I was able to manage to talk the doctor into releasing me after three days.

When I walked out of the hospital I went straight to my sister's church. She hugged me and walked me straight up to the altar and all the women began praying for me. I couldn't help but cry from the time I stepped in and Valerie put her arms around me all the way up to the front. I am not a person to cry in front of people, but I couldn't hold back. The tears just kept flowing. To tell you the truth, I cried for seven days straight, with a pause here and there. My heart was flooded with tears for days.

After that episode, I told myself that I was going to leave but I didn't go just yet. I wanted to try to see if I could make it work one more time. It didn't work, but by that time I was pregnant with my third child. I knew we were at that end of the road, but I still wanted things to work out and he didn't want to leave, so we stayed together until one night I had a funny feeling that he was doing something with my neighbor. I went over to her apartment and found myself trying to hear something with my ear to the door. I didn't hear a thing. The next thing you know, I found myself on my hands and knees, five months pregnant and peeking through a keyhole to see what they were doing. I could barely hear them, but he stayed there for hours.

I went home and told myself that it was really over this time. Days went on and something very special happened to me. I had no food and only seven dollars when I heard the voice of the Lord speak to me and tell me that he was going to bless me financially that day. I didn't know where it was going to come from, but I just felt it in my heart that something was going to happen—and it did.

My parents and I were riding down the street and we went to look at some cars. Low and behold, there was a broken down car with all the windows busted out with no plates on it, and it appeared to be abandoned. We looked inside. It appeared to be an old car that had been in an accident or had come from the junkyard. It was just sitting off to the side. My dad began getting the change off the floor, checking out the old CB that truckers use, and just generally looking over the vehicle.

Something told me to look up, and I saw a dusty manila envelope. I grabbed it and found five brand-spanking-new twenty dollar bills in it. I was so excited that I gave my father half, I took the other half, and we went straight to the grocery store. I felt so good that I came home with some food and I still had $20 left plus $5 left from the $7 that I started with. I had the $20 in my shirt and the $5 in my pocket.

When my children's father came home, I was so excited I just wanted to share with him the blessed miracle that just happened. He said, "Well, good, then give me the $20 that you have left." I said, "No!" and he said, "Give it to me!" and I moved out of his way, He proceeded to follow me and slam me up against the wall. The wind got knocked out of me. I didn't want to hit him because I was five months pregnant. So he reached in and took the money and left.

As soon as I got myself together, I began having pains in my stomach and started to dilate. The baby began trying to come down. So I got my other two daughters ready and I called a cab that charged $2.50 to get to the hospital. When I got there, they told me to calm down, and they took care of my little girls and me until I stop dilating. After some hours had passed, I was able to go home and I was fine. Thank God.

After that episode, I told that man I was leaving and I gave him 30 days to find a place. I called the landlord and told her that I was moving out. It was probably fine by her because we were always late on the rent anyway. I finally got my strength and left him. After the 30 days were up, I was gone. I moved in with my mother for three weeks and soon after I found an apartment. It was one week before Thanksgiving. I was so grateful to have my own place for the very first time. I left him alone, but of course he couldn't handle that because he felt like we should be together. But let me tell you, enough was enough. I left and I never ever looked back.

Fear

Nobody ever told me that I would have to fight my way through life to have happiness.

That's the way I see it anyway. I didn't know all of the scary things that would happen to me in this life and that they would not allow me to have the ultimate peace that I needed to survive.

Fear was the ruler of my night and the breaking of my day.

Have you ever been stalked? I sure have! Actually I've been stalked twice

The first time was when I was about 21 years of age. My children's father and I had split up, and about eight months later he decided that I didn't need my privacy anymore. To be close to me, he figured he would come over to visit the children. When I thought that he was leaving, he was crawling up into the attic out in the hallway.

I had wondered how he was getting into my apartment even after I had the locks changed. I never thought that he would do a thing like that. He knew my every move and all of my conversations with everyone who came to visit and those I talked to on the phone. I just couldn't figure out how he knew what I was doing.

One night about one o'clock in the morning, I woke up and I saw a shadow moving in my children's room. The first name that I called was his. I don't know why, but it was the first name that came out of my mouth. I quickly jumped up, because he didn't respond to the calling of his name. I began to run and heard quick and hard steps behind me. I ran even faster out into the hallway and down the stairs into my sister's apartment. I ran around her bed as fast as I could, and saw that it was my kid's father. I was scared and upset at the same time. I ran back out into the hallway and something told me to vomit. So I did, and he got scared and asked me if I was all right. I kept on vomiting, so he tried to help me up stairs. I was scared out of my wits. I walked up the stairs shaking and he kept asking if was all right.

On the one hand, I felt I shouldn't speak to him at all and just keep playing into what was happening, but on the other hand, I was paranoid. I didn't even realize that I was at knife point until I calmed down and saw the knife. He finally told me that he had been staring at me while I was sleeping and he was going kill me, that he was going to cut my throat.

I felt like this was something from a movie. When he thought that I was all right, he pressed the knife on my chest and ordered me to lie on the floor. He undressed himself from the waist down and placed the knife to my throat. Then he rape me. I didn't move because I felt so sick.

While he was still laying on me with the knife in his hand, he asked, "Do you still love me?" I lied and shook my head yes, "No, you don't," he said. "It's not the same, it feels different." Then he got up and left through the living room door.

I lay on the floor shaking uncontrollably and I couldn't get up for a while. I don't know if it was from the shock of the whole ordeal or what. How do you go from a good night's rest to being chased at knife point and then raped to gathering all of your natural thoughts like nothing ever happened? I couldn't help but wonder why he hadn't gotten the picture. I had not been with him in eight months. Why did he think it would be all right to climb up on me and take what didn't belong to him?

As such thoughts roamed in my head, I was hoping that it was all a bad dream. In reality, it was now another chapter of my painful life.

My thought about all of this is that rape is rape. The anger I carried for this man because of what he did to me was beyond a passionate hate. I never opened my door for him and he never had my permission to do what he did. Thoughts kept running through my head: What if he had killed me while I was sleep? What if my kids had woken up and found me dead? I really had a hard time dealing with this situation.

Suffering from the Attic

I was very curious about how he was getting into the house, so I went on a search of the whole premises. I checked every entryway that was visible to me and even the ones that weren't. Eventually, I looked up to the attic door. I thought to myself, "No, he wouldn't go up there, would he?" I got a chair and climbed up. I peeked my head inside and began to scan the attic. I saw my children's blanket, so I climbed all the way inside and found the spot where he had been sleeping and listening to all of my conversations. It was right over my living room. As I looked around, I began to find my bowls, blankets, forks, books and about anything else that you could name.

I decided that I was going to have to put a stop to this. I was feeling quite violated and stripped of everything that I may have thought was private, even personal matters that I may have shared with my sister—everything. After the shock wore down a little, the anger set in. After I suffered with these emotions, I began to go through the house and lock all the windows. I put new locks on my doors, and when I was done, I got a black marker and a chair and climbed back up to the attic. I put a mark on the attic, so I could tell if anyone had been in or out.

After I safely secured the house, I thought that I would feel safe, but that never happened because I began having dreams about the little black mark. I dreamed the mark was slightly moved and he was hiding in the attic again. Not only was I having trouble sleeping, but I was being tormented in my mind. I was getting up three and four times a night checking all the doors and windows and looking under every bed. There was no peace at all. Every time I had to use the bathroom I would check the shower. I could never go into a room without checking the closet—and that wasn't only at night, it was every single day. I made sure that we were going to be safe.

It got so bad that I felt this is not going to work for me, I would break down soon. I needed protection, so I went and got a gun. It was a big gun, a 44. Actually it was a pellet gun that appeared to be a real gun. All I really wanted to do was scare him when he came to try to hurt me again. I felt I couldn't go down like that anymore. He wasn't going to torture me, if I could help it.

I always called the cops on him when he harassed me in the middle of the night. They would take him down to the police station, and within a matter of hours he would be right back out and at my door, at three or four in the morning, demanding to be let in so he could see his kids. Now I was never one to deny him seeing his children at all, but I knew that this was just a scheme to get into my house. I always wondered why he would want to come to my house so late. I really never thought about it until now. All that time he was going crazy banging on my door, he was really trying to get into his sleeping quarters. The guy was secretly living with me and I didn't even know it.

When I say that I suffered at that time in my life, it was like going to hell and back and hell and back again.

Dark Places

How could you be in the light?
And still be in the dark
How can it be the beginning of day break?
And it still appears to be night
Darkness lurks upon the face of me
While light shines on them all around me
I reach out to touch the light
But it appears to be invisible
I see it but I can't touch it
I run for safety
But gloom beats me to it
Once again unsafely locked away
In darkness
Looking for a way out of these
Four walls that surround me
Will the entrapment over shadow me
Or will there be a ray of light showing through
The cracks of my hopelessness
Of these unseen walls
But as I lay at the bottom of this square
I see light, I see it, I see it
I began to scream but no one can hear me
No one can see me
I fall to the floor once again
Where the light makes its way in

I began to feel the illumination
I feel the warmth
Oh my God there is hope
God I lay
I pray
I see
I feel
Now the light seems to be more evident
The room is not so dark anymore
As I lay the light begins to fill my being
Becoming more alive
I am even able to look up
From where I am at
And see the things that scared me in the dark
And now that I see through the light
I realize that my fear was just
Unseen objects that appeared real
As I continue to lie here
With my eyes closed
I thought to myself
How can I see the light?
Without vision
So I rolled over
And I opened my eyes slowly
And to my surprise
It wasn't night anymore
It was morning

I Moved On

As all of these things were happening to me, I still had never had any counseling for all of the prior abuse in my life. I had been through so much that I felt I was going to explode. Besides all of the abuse, I went through my children's father having extra marital affairs on me. So I had all of these feelings of hurt, pain, insecurity and everything else that comes with the territory.

I wasn't ready for any type of relationship. I mean I didn't want to settle down with anyone like my last mishap, but I started talking to a young man I had known when we were in fifth grade. We were just friends at first, but eventually we became quite intimate and one thing led to the next, but still not to a real relationship because I wanted to marry a man of God who was headed the same way I wanted to go. I was a Christian, but I was in a back-sliding condition—and I still hadn't gotten over all of the garbage that I had just gone through.

I saw this big guy as an opportunity to protect me from the big bad wolf that came to hunt me down every night and torture me. So I allowed my new boyfriend to move in to protect me—and he did. Anytime that little troublemaker would come around, my new boyfriend would get at him and keep him running like he had made me run.

After a while, all of that began to die down and I began to live an almost normal life. After two years we were married and we bought a big five-bedroom house. But I was not healed from all the hurt, and I was still suffering from the tormenting fear of my last relationship. Not only that, I carried all of the insecurities of his cheating on me over into the new relationship. It was not only me; my husband was coming straight out of another relationship, too. We both had children, and we were both carrying things that hindered the relationship so that it couldn't grow properly.

We also came from two different worlds. I was a church girl and he drank, smoked weed, and gambled. I didn't do those kinds of things. But in all honesty, when I was going through all of the torment, I did begin to drink lots of beer. I felt if my ex was going to kill me, at least I would be drunk and I wouldn't feel it—or maybe I just wouldn't wake up the next morning to suffer any more torture. So my now ex-husband didn't even know why I picked up that bad habit until years later. We were just two young people getting into something without any real counsel.

I stayed with him for nine years but I have to tell you, even though he was there with me, I still never felt safe. He could protect me from the seen, but what about the unseen? I was still looking under beds and checking closets. I would get very upset when the front door wasn't locked. I was still suffering with fear of the other guy. So I purchased another gun. This one was a little gun, a 22, but this one was real. I got a small one because I had small children in the house and I didn't want to be too obvious. I know it was a crazy move, but there were some things that my ex did to me that night that I can't even write about. Just know for the sake of my children, I've held some things back.

The marriage that I was now in was a rebound relationship. It ceased after the nine years expired. That was a hard thing for me to do, but after the first four or five years the whole marriage went downhill. I don't want to say bad things about that relationship, but what I will tell you I learned to never marry unequally yoked and to have more things in common than sex. Make sure the other person is just not fulfilling a temporary need and can cover you for the rest of your days. Make sure he or she can pray you through situations and not sex you through them. The highs of sex wear off and you are left dealing with the same situation that you started with. My advice is to seek real counsel from a pastor or someone in the fold.

There was lots of unresolved hurt in that relationship, both his garbage and mine. After a long time, we both apologized to each other and realized our own mistakes. We accepted them and, though it was very hard, we moved on.

I'll tell you another thing I've learned. I took out a lot of "me time" before I even looked at another man. I took three years before I even went on a date. "Me time" is a wonderful thing. I learned so much about myself. There was no more hurt being applied to my life, just healing of past wounds. I began to take control over my life with good sound counsel and lots of people praying for me and with me. I finally overcame the fear that caused me to constantly keep checking my locked doors and it has been years since I looked in a closet or shower or anything like that. I thought it would never cease, but it did.

I moved out of the big five-bedroom house and down into a place that wasn't the greatest, but I got down there and I fixed that place up like I lived in a penthouse. It was mine, and over the years I found that I had more peace in that place then I ever had in my entire life. No one hurting me, no more pain, no attics.

It was just my children and me. It's kind of funny, I was used to someone lying behind me when I slept, so I found myself sleeping on the couch for three years. I hadn't realized that the couch had a sense of support. I always felt comforted. Sounds crazy, but it worked for me.

Girls and guys, you deserve some "me time" and if I were you, I would take it as soon as possible. Enjoy yourself as much as you can in this life because no one is going to do it for you. Life does get better when you have a clear mind. Trust me. How do you think that I can sing and make CD's and write books? It took a lot of "me time" to find out that I had self worth.

Another Form of Healing for Me

This is about the neighbor who never missed anything.

Sometimes our blessings come in disguise, and I never thought that the woman I met when she walked into my job at All-State to get insurance would be my saving grace. I didn't know that two years later she would become my next door neighbor. She never knew what had happened in the past to make me have this fear inside. I never told her that I was afraid to live alone. This is how it happened. She was nosey, and I was scared. She never missed a thing and I always looked over my shoulder. For the years that I lived there, she always stood outside on that balcony and watched everything and everybody. She knew every car that came into the complex, and if she didn't know she would ask. She always knew what time I left and what time I came in. If I had a play or something she would say in her Puerto Rican voice, "You came in late last night, Missy," and she would tell me who came to my door looking for me.

I kept my screen door locked all night and I left the storm glass in all year round in place of the screen. I didn't want anyone cutting the screen and breaking into my apartment. I lived on the third floor and this was the only way in and the only way out. The woman who one might call nosey helped me to sleep at night because of her presence outside of my door. She never really went anywhere, so she was always home. I was also home a lot, but there were times when I had to be out of town for shows and so forth. I felt really safe and comfortable with her being the neighbor that didn't let anything get past her. I needed that time and that space to learn all over again what it was like to be in total peace. We lived next door to each other for five years.

Who would have ever thought that the woman you would call nosey would have been accepted into a housing development the same month that I was moving out. We were both packing at the same time. We were each going into our new destiny. God's mission for that task was over. He never let her move until I was totally healed in my inner man. There were plenty of apartments that she was getting accepted for, but they always fell through.

God wouldn't let her move because he knew that I still needed her. When we both found out that we were moving on with our lives, we were both very happy, and none of this was planned. Life is quite funny. We don't know who is really for you and who's not. She was a total stranger and after some years I found her to be my anchor through God in the midst of my storm.

To you Flaheta: I love you, and thanks for being the neighbor that watched it all.

Has Anyone Seen Him?

I once asked the question, "Has anyone seen my lover? He is chocolate and ruddy, and he left me in the middle of the night."

When I stopped to ask the guard, "Where is he?" I got whipped. She said, "I've seen him. He's been with me."

Have you ever had a woman confront you about the man that you love? I have. She told me that she had been with my man and he told her that he never loved me. My heart was ripped, stripped and dipped in a pot of hot oil. It killed me to hear her say that she kissed him and that he touched her in places that only married people should be touched. For my lover was all I had, I thought. He was my heart.

But today I thank God for the word "was." Those past-tense words have great meaning. Today, I no longer take beatings for love and I have no evident scars from the man that I called my lover.

To the lady who laughed at me when she thought she had

my lover, I say: "What goes around comes around. I'll pray for you that God has mercy on you that you will not have to suffer the way that I did."

To the man who betrayed me and my pure love, I say: "Your past is going to catch up with you in your future, but my deliverance comes in where I never tried to get you back. Now I am happier than ever, and it is killing you to see someone else treat me the way that you should have. It will hurt you more in the long run than it has hurt me. Thanks for sleeping with the guard, because it showed me where your love really was."

Just a Thought

Somebody sang the song, "who wrote the book on love" and I say, if you ever find them please send them to me there are a few things we need to chat about.

The Let Downs of Love

Have you ever loved someone so much that it hurts? I really did love someone like that and because we could never hook up in a sense, I decided to let it go. They always say that you can't miss what you've never had. But I say that's a lie, because you don't have to actually have something to want it badly. It's like a fantasy that you live out in your head every day. Sometimes I felt like I was on a drug or something and trying to refrain from my next high. As I tried to let go of this man, I began going through withdrawal, and I can tell you that it doesn't feel good at all.

Have you ever just laid in your bed hoping that the next call would be him or maybe he would be surprising you at the front door—kind of like a story out of a book? It was so hard trying to get my drug of love off my mind, but some days it just seemed like he was sinking into my spirit deeper and deeper. I could feel my inner self crying. I heard it calling, "Somebody, anybody, can you stop the pain? Please can you stop the pain?"

I wasn't making this thing up in my head. This man did claim that he wanted to marry me, so I kept the thought in my heart for a very long time. He told me that there was nothing more in life that he wanted than for me to be his wife. I waited for him to do what he promised, but he never made good on it. I felt strung along because I truly believed that he loved me. I also felt played with, that my emotions were being tampered with.

Have you been in a place where you were in love with someone and while you were alone or on the telephone with him, you were the center of his attention? He would say things to you that you had been longing to hear and everything seemed sweet, but as soon as you got in front of a crowd, he wouldn't give you the same attention. You watched as he went through his own little ritual of "I am alone. I am not attached to anyone." You had to kind of stand back, make fake phone calls, or act like your phone was ringing to make yourself feel important—like "I don't need you. I've got other people calling me." Then as soon as you walked in your front door at home and it's convenient for him, he calls, "Hey, Baby…." And being so desperate for love, we just let go and take the call anyway, feeling that one day he will realize what a wonderful woman you are.

It's all a lie! He will never come to the conclusion that you are the best for them. If he is hiding you, it means that he is on the prowl for something else. And sure enough, with me that's exactly what happened. He ended up with five other women as he held on to my cooked dinners, my gifts, my time, and my energy.

Another guy did the same exact thing to me. He strung me along for the longest time and kept telling me that he was waiting on God to see if I was his wife. I waited right along with him, holding on while ignoring all the signs that he was sneaky. When he dumped me and married someone else, he had a great alibi, because he had told people that we were only friends.

Have you ever wanted something so bad and couldn't have it? Well, not anymore, I thought. I cried out to God for His hand of grace to help me through this, and as soon as I would get a handle on it, I was right back in love again. I named it, I claimed it and I put his name on a piece of paper and put it in the fire, and I said no more. But none of it helped me. Every time I tried to conquer this thing, there he was, showing up out of nowhere. How could I resist that?

Why is it that when we love, we love hard and when we lose,

we lose even harder? I believe it's because of the chase. When you chase something with everything in you, it's only when the chase is over that you realize how tired you are. You are totally exhausted. Now you are ready to collapse, and you have no energy for anything or anyone. And they are still hiding you and their relationship with you. They tell everyone around you, "Yes, she is a very nice person." But that's it; it's clear from those words that there is no real commitment. Your best friend is the only one who knows the real truth and maybe a few others, but not by his choice.

If we sought God first on these situations, he would tell us the truth and we wouldn't get caught up in this stuff. Do you think God would send you the mate of your life and hide him from you, like the game of hide and seek? No, God doesn't play mind games; that's for immature individuals who don't know the voice of the Lord. They may act like they know, but if you are being strung along with no real answer, that is a mind game. You are the board and anytime he feels like picking up his pieces he will, and without an apology. He will thank God for his new blessing and dance and shout right in your face. The really bad thing about these situations is that you give all of your love to someone who is not giving you the love that you deserve while there is someone out there that wants to love you with every part of his being. What's more, because of your chase, you are too tired and wounded from all the falls to see fresh love right in front of you.

Finally after a good long while and a good long look at my situation and my life, I gave up on the lust that I thought was love. God told me in his word that I was a lit city on a hill, for all to see—and from now on, I was not going to be hid. Anyone who was going to love me would see me the same way. I started realizing that love would not hurt me, but a person would. That day was a new day in my life and I was ready for new love and I believed that he would come and he would come strong. I believed that he would love me unconditionally. When he said that he would marry me, he would mean it.

Just My Thoughts Again…
Has anyone ever told you, if you love something, let it go

And if it returns to you, it was meant to be?

Well somebody lied. There was something that I let go of And when it tried to return, I didn't want anything to do with it I'm just a little curious, was that love Or Was it that he was no good for me and I needed a waste basket To get rid of the trash? Hmm.

CHAPTER 7

Things Began to Turn Around

After the second breakup of the nine-year relationship, I was sitting on the floor crying and upset over all that was taking place. I was about to give up my five-bedroom house, I didn't have an apartment to live in, and I couldn't handle my ex seeing another woman. As I sat on the floor, I began to pray, asking God for direction. I was thirty at the time and I felt like I had nothing. It was just my children and me once again, but this time I decided ahead of time that I would do things a lot differently.

I heard a voice tell me to look in the Yellow Pages, so I started flipping through the telephone book, finding little things here and there that meant nothing to me until I came to a place called Aural Gratifications. I picked the telephone up and dialed the number with a little ray of hope.

I heard a man's voice say, "Hello, Aural Gratifications."

I said, "Hello, my name is Michelle and I am a gospel singer. I was just wondering if you would have use of my service."

To my surprise, he said, "Yes, we are in the process of doing a jingle for Strawberries music store and we need a good strong voice," he said. "Why don't you send us a tape and we'll listen to your voice. If we're interested, we'll give you a call."

I told him that I didn't have a CD. All I had was a little tape recorder. He said that was OK, to send it anyway. I told him I would, and he took my phone number. Then we hung up.

I called the bank that owned my house and told them that they could have it back because I wouldn't be living here anymore. They told me if I would clean the house out, they would give me the amount I needed to move into my next apartment. I got excited because I had no money for an apartment or any security money.

I immediately jumped up off of the floor and went out in search of a place. I had a friend who knew a rental agent and put in a good word for me. Within a week, I had landed an apartment.

I called the bank back and told them what I needed and they cut me a check for $1,000 dollars. Actually, I was $200 short, but that was no problem because I got that from my father. Old Dad came to my rescue. Shortly after, I moved into my new place.

Two months later I got a call from Aural Gratifications asking me if I'd sent the tape. I told them no, and they asked me to get it to them as soon a possible as they needed it within that week. I told them I would and took all the information again. I went to a friend by the name of Aaron Lacey who played a tune for me that I heard in my head. I put a few words to it and taped it on the little tape recorder.

The very next day, I placed it in the mailbox. I wasn't all that excited because not many good things had ever happened for me. But I listened to the voice of the Lord and it paid off. Within a few days my phone rang and it was Kevin Bartlette from Aural Gratifications.

"Michelle," he said, "you are our girl. We love your voice." I mean they were ranting and raving over me. He asked if we could meet early the next week. I couldn't believe it! I got all excited and told him yes. He gave me directions and I made my way there.

Within the first few months of my doing Strawberries, Aural Gratifications called a meeting. I went in and sat down with the team in Kevin's office. They wanted to let me know that our commercial had come in first place in a jingle competition and that we won an award for the performance. They told me that the way I sang and the little laugh I did in the jingle had caught the attention of the judges and they had been very pleased. I was the one pleased to hear such a thing!
They looked at each other with a smile and said, "Would you be our Strawberries girl?"

"Me?" I asked, happily. "This can't be true! You want me? I mean, come on, I just started singing a little over three years ago. I haven't sung anywhere besides church and at home, and now you want my voice all over radio and television?" It didn't take me long to say yes. I felt so honored.

They told me that I was easy to work with because I knew all of the various harmonies. Now that was hard to believe because I tried to join a singing group at the age of twenty, and they kicked me out in the first rehearsal and told me to never come back. My sister and I had asked to sing in the group, and they were all excited and told us to come to their practice that very night. They loved my sister's voice, but as soon as I opened my mouth to sing that first song, I couldn't hold a note to save my life and I jumped from one key to another. I guess I was tone deaf. My sister knew that I couldn't sing. She would tell me to shut up, and stop singing, that I was making her sick.

Now someone was telling me something very different. I thank God for the desire to sing, because God showed up and gave me what I wanted most: a voice to sing. Not long after that, I did more and more jingles and from there sang back up for an up-and-coming artist. Things were just flowing and the money wasn't bad at all. It helped to pay all my bills. I thought that I had arrived. I was feeling good, no more arguing with a man, no more being hurt, no one cursing and swearing at me. I was getting my children in line. I mean, things were really looking up. See, when you have a clear head about yourself, you can achieve the world. I went to work every day to support us with the help of God.

Not long after, I was asked to play a big part in a musical play called "Don't Let the Devil Ride" written by Jimmy and Ralphine Childs in which I played a jealous wife. Now that was right up my alley! I did it very well because I was a good actress. I loved to fall in and out of character long before a play. Acting was a form of fun for me, and I made people laugh all the time with my different roles and funny dances, which made me happy, too. I traveled in that play for a while. I never got to go anywhere except church and church functions, and now I was starting to see a little something of the world and I loved every minute of it.

I entered a music contest to write a Christmas song that had to be less than three minutes. Well, guess what? I won first place! I felt so good; I was finally winning in life. I started working at a place called Mortgage Select and became one of their top junior mortgage loan officers. I moved up three positions in one year, and all three with pay increases. I was doing so well that my heart was healing, and things kept getting better and better.

One day at work, I heard the voice of the Lord tell me to take a break and walk down the street. When I dressed that morning, the Lord had told me to put on a certain dress and the high heel shoes that I had worn to my brother's wedding. I had vowed to never wear them again because they made me feel so tall. I am already tall but those shoes made me look six feet tall. As I was walking listening to God's voice, he told me to walk with my head up high. I thought it couldn't get any higher than that! Nah, just kidding—but he told me to keep my head up because I was going to meet someone. I started walking down Wall Street in Kingston and a rather short man looked up at me and said hello and with a pleasant smile I said hello right back as we passed each other.

He came running back and looked at me and asked, "Do you act?" and I said yes. He asked, "Do you sing?" I said yes.

"Please don't move," he said, "I have someone that I need for you to meet." He ran into my favorite store called Richard the First, now called Columbia, and grabbed a lady by the hand, saying, "I found her! I found her!"

I stood there like, "You found who?"

He brought the lady out and introduced me. "This is Gillian Farrell, the woman that I need you to meet." To Gillian, he said, "She acts and she sings." She explained to me that they were looking for an actress to play the part of Sojourner Truth and asked me if I could come up for an audition on Saturday. I told her sure. I felt like, "OK, I like this, but I still haven't auditioned yet so I don't want to get too excited."

I went up to Woodstock that Saturday to an old barn for the audition. Gillian asked me to read a script for her. I looked at it and began to read. She said not to worry about the reading for now. There was a little song in there called, "I Know I've Been Changed."

"I have never heard of it before, have you?" she asked.

This was becoming very interesting. I didn't know a lot of songs, because I had only been singing for a few years, but this was my favorite because I really had been changed from all of the hate that I had in my life. God had changed it to love. "Yes," I told her, "I do know this song," and it happens to be my favorite. She sat down and said, "Whenever you're ready."

I was nervous, but I closed my eyes like I always do and I began to sing a cappella. When I finished the song, I opened my eyes and Gillian was sitting there crying. She was not crying little tears either; there were big happy tears streaming down her face.

I didn't understand why anyone would cry over the way that I sang, but strangely it was something that started happening to me wherever I went.

She walked over to me and said, "I would be honored if you would play the part of Sojourner." I was shocked. We hugged and chatted a little, and then she gave me the script of about 48 pages that I was to learn in three weeks. Little did I know that she had already put a production team together and they had already been working on this play. They just couldn't find a Sojourner, which was the lead role. Oh my goodness, the pressure was on!

Another ironic aspect of this was that six months prior, there had been a casting call for a Sojourner. Elder Sandra HopGood told me to get in touch with her friend Steven Gottlieb and get the script and check it out. "I think you are the one for this part," she had told me. I sent for the script but when I saw how many pages I was suppose to learn immediately, I threw it in the garbage. I could never learn all of those words. Elder Hopgood did ask me about it, but I told her I just couldn't do it, and never thought about it again.

Now here I was, standing with the same script in my hand.

I thought, "God, you must have a purpose and a plan. This was ordained by you." I studied the script over and over and I had no luck at all. I was frustrated because now they were selling tickets and the play was sold out. I was at rehearsal every single night for those three weeks. The best thing about the script was that I was supposed to sing in between some of the lines, and that made it easy because I knew a lot of church hymns. After toiling over the script, I lay down one night and prayed for God to help me. I fell asleep and as I slept, all the words started coming down into me in this black and white form. It was like my mind was having dinner, eating everything that fell from up above.

I woke up the next morning and called Gillian and said, "I got it, I really got it!" I went to rehearsal that night and I had it all down to the last word. The play went forth. I believe we had two or three shows set up for that weekend. It was a smash hit, and my picture was posted on all kinds of newspapers. And it didn't stop there. We took the play from city to city. The best part was that I took my children along with me, and they were even allowed to play parts in the play.

It was awesome. Old, young, and in between were crying and thanking me for opening their eyes to this kind of inhumane treatment. Sojourner Truth was a woman who was freed from slavery, and she went through all the trials of a slave from her son being sold to being beaten with a whip by her master. It was a very emotional play, and I threw myself into it just as if Sojourner were me, because as I played the part she was me. She was abused just like I was. She was raised in Kingston and sold when she was nine-years old down by the Rondout where I grew up. She was beaten and misused. She loved hard and ended up with a broken heart. There was a monument of her right across the street from my job, which I never noticed. She fought and won her son back at the court right across the street from my job. I looked out that window everyday and never even knew that Sojourner's life was right in my face.

I don't think they could have found a better person to play her part. I know for sure I was called to do that particular work. After all of her saga, she was known for her singing and her writing and her preaching. She loved the children and always looked out for them. That's the same thing I do. I had a children's choir and I am currently working in a high school.

Life had really begun to flourish for me. After all of this happened, I heard the Lord's voice again telling me to leave my job. I said, "God, are you sure? I can't do that! How am I going to take care of my family? I am the only one here for them. I don't get any child support."

He told me that he had it all under control and I said, "Well, if you make a way, then I will leave." There was a woman on my job who always caused problems. She came up to me one day and said, "If you don't like your job, then why don't you just quit?" I looked at her as if to say, "Thank you. I will do just that." I walked into my boss's office, shook his hand, told him thanks for the opportunity—and I left.

I had three prophesies pertaining to my leaving. God sent two people that I didn't even know and another that I hadn't seen in years. They all came to me at the same time. I left the job and I called Gillian who told me, "That's good. We are going to put you on a stipend and will pay you once a month plus still pay you for your plays." I was so happy.

That same week I got a letter from Section 8, a rental subsidy, saying they had knocked my rent all the way down to $114 a month. They told me they don't know how I even got a call. I told them I was on the waiting list for three years. They said, "Yes, we know but we don't understand how you got a call because you are a P2. I asked what a P2 was. They told me that would be someone who has a job with my kind of money. I wasn't making a lot, but I guess they figured if I had made it this long, I could continue to make it. I told her, "Well, lady, I don't have a job, I just lost it."

She said, "Okay, that makes you a P1." Immediately I was placed on the list.

I was so impressed with God. I was wondering how he did that. I had never even gotten a call from the housing people in 3 years, but the same week that I left the job, I got a call and got accepted. Wow! This was beyond me.

Now I had lots of time to practice plays and learn the new ones that we were putting on. I was also ready to make my own CD. Between Gillian, my church, and a benefit concert with lots of donations, I was able to raise $4,000 and some change. I was officially a gospel recording artist. I sometimes still can't believe how God just turned my life around for my good.

From there, I started going down to audition for Broadway shows like The Color Purple, Hairspray and all kinds of things. Before you knew it, I was meeting stars left and right. I was in all kinds of newspapers. I was singing and being interviewed on several different television shows, including on TBN. By then I felt that the sky was the limit for me. God only knows where I am going next, but I do know this, God has definitely got his hand upon my life.

Chapter 8

Why My Parents Hurt Me

I truly believe that there is a reason why people act the way that they do. I always wondered why my parents were as crazy as they were when I was growing up. I am going to take you on a small journey through their lives and maybe you will be able to see how and why your parents or just some people in your life act or have acted the way that they do.

Let's start with my father, who was an only child. He grew up in a nice neighborhood and had a very loving family. His grandparents, whom he loved dearly, raised him because—get this—his mother told him that she was his sister. For about twelve years he called his mother by her first name, which was Amy. One day in the midst of a heated conversation someone told him that Amy was his mother, not his sister. From what I understand, from that time on, he and his mother never got along. He could never respect her as his mother. The relationship with her was based on a lie.

As time passed, the man that I knew as my father continued to build the relationship with his grandmother, whose name was Cora. Still very confused, my father was quite angry. Regardless, he still loved his grandmother. One day Cora was sitting in her living room and she asked my father to go to the store for her, so he went. To him, it was just like any other day when she had asked him to do something for her. He got up and obediently went to the store.

When he came back with her request, he told her, "Here, Momma," but she didn't respond. She just sat straight up looking as if she were sleep. My dad tried to wake her up, but she just wouldn't get up. He got his grandfather to try to wake her up and she still didn't respond. They called an ambulance and found out that she had died of a massive heart attack. My father was the one who found her dead. He then was forced to be with the woman whom he considered betrayed him. He still called her Amy, because as stubborn as he was, that was never going to change. I never heard him call his mother "Mom."

My dad eventually joined the army and became a paratrooper. He jumped out of planes and really enjoyed being a daredevil. This was a man who didn't have a fear in the world! He probably would have been a great contestant for the show "Fear Factor." My dad was enjoying life as a young man should—until he had to go to war.

He never liked to talk about the war, but from what I got from him, I can see why his life took a turn for the worse. He told me that when he went to war that he had to kill men, women and children—people who had never done anything to him—and he couldn't live with the guilt. He said over there, it was either kill or be killed, but the pictures of killing the innocent women and kids still flashed through his head. He said it would be like us sitting in our own living room and someone kicking in the door and just shooting all of us for nothing.

So my father began to drink quite heavily to cover the pain. That, of course, was not the answer because he only caused more pain to those around him. He began to live quite recklessly and made lots of children along the way. I've never met them, but maybe he was trying to replenish some of the children that he had taken out during war. Who really knows? I do know that I have lots of half sisters and brothers over in Korea, and a few here in New York. My father met my mother and she had a few hang ups of her own. My father was used to getting any woman that he wanted, so when he met my mother, he asked her to get into his car so he could give her a ride home and she declined. That really shocked him because as handsome as he was, that just wasn't the response that he was looking for. Because she wouldn't give him the time of day, he hunted her down and married her.

(Girls, remember this: if you don't remember anything else: men love a challenge.)

My parents began a life of having children immediately. Their first son was named Raymond David Cook. I came along a year later, and then my brother Jay was born. It was just us three for a while.

Finally a Happy Family—Or Was It?

My family began as any normal family would: we were born and brought home from the hospital. From there everything became abnormal. Some crazy things began to take place. My father and my oldest brother, Raymond, became very close, and my father's real mother, my grandmother, took to him as though he belonged to her. As time went on, my brother was diagnosed with some kind of illness that no one thought was dangerous. He was in the hospital off and on and my father and my brother began to bond as any father and son would.

My father went way out of his way to buy Raymond all kinds of presents because he was sick so often. I recall my father coming through the door with a wrapped present for him, and I would think, "Where is mine?" It didn't really matter because I knew they were just trying to make him happy.

One day my father went to the hospital to see the young man that was named after him, his first real son that he could spend time with and the young man that the schools considered a genius. Raymond was his heart and everybody knew it. He had been sick for about three months, but my father thought that he was getting better and that he would be coming home later on that week. But when he walked in, my sweet brother said to my father, "I waited for you, Daddy, I knew you were coming and he grabbed my dad's hand and they exchanged a smile. My seven-year-old brother died holding my father's hand.

Why My Parents Hurt Me

His death was not expected. We thought he was coming home. I had toys for him. We had planned a surprise party for his arrival.

"Somebody tell me what is happening," my father must have thought. This had to knock my father for a loop and a half. How was he supposed to deal with this and us? From that time on, my father became very distant toward me. I think he probably only did that because he was afraid to love a person who might die, like his grandmother and his son had done. His anger began to kick in from all the earlier hurts.

When people ask me how I could forgive my father for all the abuse, I say "only through Christ," but looking back over his past, I am blessed just to be alive. Someone might ask where my mother was during all of the physical abuse. It's time to go on a journey of my mother's life.

Hello, Mamma

My mother's life started out quite shabbily, too. She was born on November 2, 1942, and she was always told that her father hadn't wanted her. She grew up with her brothers and sisters and at the age of fourteen, her mother died. Around that same time, she became pregnant with my oldest sister, Rose. Back in those days, she was considered an unwed mother. She said that she really wanted to be with the baby's father, but because he was nineteen and she was fourteen, he was put in jail for statutory rape. She never thought it was rape because she loved him.

She was put into a group home for girls and the baby was allowed to stay with her for one year. She would be allowed to take the baby home with her if a family member would take her in, but of course no one would. So the baby was removed from her. That is a lot of loss for a fifteen-year-old girl. They had put her in a school called Wassaic, because back in those days there were few places that took in young pregnant girls. There were also mentally retarded girls there, and that's all my mother knew for quite a while.

She never learned to read and she could barely write. When she came out of that place she was wounded and just thrown to the dogs. No education and no real place to go. She had family in the south and an aunt in New York City, but no one took her in.

She ended up in Kingston where Wassaic had sent her. She tried to get her life together but it was very hard. Wassaic told her that if she married, she would be able to get her daughter back. So when she met my father and they married, she thought everything was going to be wonderful. It wasn't. Suddenly Wassaic couldn't find her daughter. They said the adoption agency lost all records of the child. Wow! My mother's dreams were just shattered all over again. She decided to go ahead and have some more children.

When my brother was born that bought her great joy. He was wonderful and very smart. She was finally beginning to move on with her life while continuing to look for her daughter. She was still living with an alcoholic, which wasn't the best of life, but it was better than being homeless.

She thought that life couldn't get any worse and then my father called from the hospital to tell her that my brother had just died unexpectedly. My mother carried the burden so strongly because she had a sickle cell trait, and my father blamed my mother, saying that she killed their son with that trait. Although it wasn't true, just imagine losing your first son and hearing this kind of garbage from the man who should be comforting you.

My mom sunk into a deep depression. After the funeral, she said she couldn't sleep because she kept thinking that my brother was in the ground freezing. She felt like he could not get warm, like he was cold and she could not keep him warm. She was badly tortured for a long time. She felt she couldn't do anything right anymore.

Finally one day when my other brother, Jay, and I were in the living room playing, she felt Raymond's spirit come into the room and hover over us. He told her to stop worrying about him and that he was not cold. When she told me this, I believed her because I saw my brother in the room with us and I was only six at the time. I remember it as clear as day.

After that my mother was able to go on. Although I was the next child in line, I began to feel neglected. I began to be hollered at and abused a lot more than normal. I guess because my mother lost her son, she needed to bond to another son child. So I was skipped over and my mother began to bond with my brother who she spoiled rotten. He wasn't spoiled by my dad, however, because I don't think that he was ready to give love to anyone at that time.

These two wounded people were trying to raise the rest of us children with all of their unhealed cuts that never had a band-aid. They were leaking blood all over the place, and I was covered in it.

Was it fair? No. Was it my fault that I was put through all of this stuff? No.

My parents needed counseling and they needed it badly. My father began to have extra marital affairs and I knew about most of them. My mother took on a relationship that she had to hide. She said he was just a friend, but that's not what I saw. All of this confusion in our house contributed to my father's alcoholic friends coming in and fondling me, and maybe one of my little sisters. I am not sure.

Eventually these two people did get their lives together and they went their own separate ways. When I got older, I was able to reap the benefits of having really great parents, but it still left me very wounded. I had to work out all of the kinks in my life, but I figured if they could do it, then so could I.

No Grandma, No Love

I often wondered why Grandma gave all of her love to my first brother and never to any of the rest of us, except my younger brother, Jay, after Raymond died. Now that I am older I am trying to analyze the situation. Was it because she wasn't the proper kind of parent to her own child who despised her? Was it that by giving all of that love to my brother she felt she was making up for all the mistakes that she made with my father? Was it that she needed a second chance at life with her grandson to make him feel like a son? Was it because her mother parented her son for her and she wanted to walk in her own mother's shoes? What? What was it that made her so mean to the rest of us children?

She had lots of money and I don't remember her spending anything on us, ever. Maybe after placing all of that love on my sweet brother, it was a big letdown for her when he died, and she was afraid to love anyone else. In hindsight, she did have a very hard time with the loss of my brother. Whenever anyone mentioned his name, she would just break down and cry. This happened until I was in my twenties.

She mourned his death for years, but I think it went deeper than just his death, because her mother died and I never heard her cry about that. All I ever heard her say was, "My little Snooky. He was as wonderful as they come." I think that she felt less of a woman because she couldn't save him with her love. She became bitter toward all of us because if she allowed herself to love one of us again, we just might die. I can't really pinpoint her reasons, but she was very harsh on us as children. She never let her guard down—not for one minute.

As I got older, I was hurt by her rejection. I borrowed fifty cents from her one time and I never lived it down. She told a friend whose garbage I used to take out as a child that I owed her fifty cents and she wanted it and she would never give me anything else again. Wow! What kind of grandmother was that? I could never figure it out. I couldn't wait to pay her back her little fifty cents. I always wondered why my father always stressed that he wanted to be paid back, and now I know why he was that way.

Life is very funny how it takes turns on you. My grandmother had a stroke when I was seventeen. My father called me, and I rushed to him. We called the ambulance and got her to the hospital. I stayed by my father's side the whole time. She got through it, but a few years later she had another one. Who got called? Me, of course. I went without any hesitation just like before.

This time I stayed in the hospital with her while she lay there mumbling words that I didn't understand. Finally I heard her say 1977, and those were her last words. I watched her slip into a coma. I later found out that 1977 was the year her beloved husband died. I stood there looking at this woman who hated me for no apparent reason. I unraveled her hair and combed it. It was long, black and pretty. I thought she has the prettiest hair, and the nicest red skin that I had ever seen. She was an Indian. She was a very attractive woman, but still so mean. She carried all of that with her to her grave.

I never thought that I would be the one that would be there with her in her last days. Before she slipped into the coma, she took the cross that hung from her necklace and rubbed it as fast and hard as possible across her chest. Maybe she was asking God for redemption. I wasn't sure; I couldn't judge the matter at hand.

What I will always remember about my grandmother was that she was not the type of person that I would ever want to be. I made it my business not to entertain all the neighbors' children and make them smile and then come into the house and not keep that same smile. Everyone on the block loved my grandmother. She gave them candy and they all called her Grandma Ross. They had more of a relationship with her than any of us ever did. Wow, what a pity!

Maybe it's not for me to figure out. Maybe this was just one of life's lessons on how and what not to do to the people you are supposed to love. Take it from me, Lesson One was well learned. Thanks, Grandma. Thanks a lot.

My Thought Exactly
I thank God for the people who accept me for the person that I am
And not for the person that I am not
So
Just love me for who I am
And accept me for who I am not

CHAPTER 9

I Tried to Drink and Puff

I went through so much as a child that I even tried to smoke marijuana twice and that didn't work. It made me feel like the blood rushed from the top of my head to the souls of my feet. I mean I just knew that I was going to die. I started hallucinating and everything. I told God, "If you get me through this, I will never do it again," and that was one promise that I was glad to keep.

After that I started drinking beer. I felt so happy inside because I thought that I found my one true friend that was going to keep me happy. Beer became the best thing that ever happened to me. I loved the taste and I loved how it made me feel. And that was wonderful to me. I needed something to cover the pain I was suffering through. I had no support group, no one holding my hand, and no one telling me that everything was going to be all right. So I did what I thought was right.

I had been drinking beer for solace for about a year when all of a sudden I felt God never wanted me to drink anyway because of my ministry. Alcohol couldn't be part of it. Suddenly the beer became like water. I would drink it, but it wouldn't make me feel good. I tried and tried and nothing worked. I looked up at God and I was kind of angry. I said, "I finally found something that began to take away some of my pain and that I thought was helping me to feel better in life and now you are taking it away. Now what is it that I am going to do?"

So I prayed to God about the situation and He began to show himself worthy to me so that I didn't even want to drink anymore. Wow, what a transition to go through! What had I been thinking? What would make me drink beer knowing that my father was the man that he was due to his drinking? Maybe I wasn't thinking. Maybe he drank to escape his pain and he was not strong enough at the time to stop. God didn't want me to take the same path that my father took.

I realized something about myself as I began to write this book. When I was a little girl, I could never tell anyone anything about the abuse that I was suffering. Not one soul. Even though the neighbors knew, there seemed to be no hope for me when it was occurring.

One day I decided to seek help by telling the nurse about the beating that I had received that morning before going to class. I was beaten with an extension cord and I had bruises all over my body. The nurse bought me home and asked my mother about the beating.

My mother looked me straight in the face and said, "I didn't do that to her."

She then asked me, "Why you are lying on me."

She then turned to the nurse and said, "Maybe her father hit her, but it wasn't me."

The nurse then ordered my father to be removed from the home if I were to continue to live there. I heard my mom tell my dad that I had told on him and he needed to leave and he left. I wasn't mad that he left, because back then all he did was drink and beat me anyway. I was mad, though, at my mom for always using me as the scapegoat for everything. It wasn't fair.

He eventually was allowed back into the home and believe you me, he got me for that! It seemed I could never live it down. I vowed to myself to never tell anything else again. I kept all kinds of things inside until I couldn't hold any more. When you don't release the hurt in life, it will seep out one way or another. That's how I ended up having a nervous breakdown.

Once during the time when I was in the relationship with my children's father, I cried sometimes even when nothing bad was happening to me. I guess I was severely depressed. He made a statement to me that made me not want to cry anymore. He called me a crybaby. Since all I wanted to do was please him anyway, I dried up my tears, but I began to ache inside even more.

I didn't know why I was crying like that anyway, until the nervous breakdown. When it happened, I was on the altar crying and a sister Carolyn came over and began hugging me. I began pouring out. I cried and cried and cried and she said to me, "I didn't know it was that bad for you."

I told her about the relationship, how bad it was and about how I was starving, eating rice and cheese. I told her about the extra marital affairs that I had been dealing with and so forth. That was the first time I told anything about myself since the school nurse. I was starving in the house but wouldn't ask for $10 from my family for food. I would rather go to a food pantry then to tell anything negative about my family.

For anyone out there holding things in, don't do it. The only person that suffers is you.

After breaking my silence, I talked and talked and cried and talked to where I couldn't stop talking. After a while I was telling all of my business, your business and everyone else's business because I couldn't help myself. It seemed like I was releasing. I thought I was healing, but in reality I was healing myself while hurting others.

It never dawned on me until one day a good friend said to me, "You know, you can't even hold water. If you had a cup of water, it would tip." He said this to me on more than one occasion and it really hurt my feelings, because I just wanted to be wanted, loved and accepted.

At first I got really mad at him and thought. "Who does he think he is? Why does he think he can say that about me and get away with it." Then reality set in and I began to question myself. I finally realized that he was being a real friend because only real people tell you the truth about yourself, and then it's up to you to work on it.

I went to bed that night and I prayed and asked God why was I this way, when did it start and how I could fix it. He began to show me myself from a child, and everything began to become much clearer for me. I saw what I was doing and how it was hurting others as well as myself. I asked the Lord to help me to stop what I was doing and to change me.

And he did just that. I couldn't undo what was already done, but I got up the next morning and started right from there, one day at a time, and before I knew it, I was not talking about anyone at all and I still felt healthy. I had never meant to hurt anyone, but they say those who hurt sometimes hurt others and I am very sorry. What's meant to be told will be told and what's not won't be. Thank you, God, for deliverance. Today I am truly free from the bondage that was holding me.

(11 Years Ago, I said these words)

Who Can Love Me?

Besides God,
Who can love this woman?
Who is so full of love?
Yes I'm full of pain
Yes I've been hurt
Yes I think real hard
And yes I study things
No, nothing gets past me
And yes sometimes I just shut down
But
I love me
And I want me to be loved
I give so much in life
But I don't receive the love
That I am searching for
Lord who will love me
Please help me to be loved for real.

Failed But Not a Failure

I failed 7th grade 3 times. It wasn't because I was dumb; it was because I didn't have anyone to believe in me. I continued to spiral out of control with my behavior and my disciplinary list grew thicker and thicker. I had turned into an angry child. I never remember my parents coming to any of my plays, my school meetings, or anything else; so, I knew that when I got into trouble they wouldn't come to the school then either. One thing

I know now is that I was never dumb. If I'd just had someone push me and believe in me, I would've been somewhere great. Even though I failed 7th grade 3 times and got pushed up to the 8th grade, I dropped out. But, just because you are a drop-out that doesn't mean that you can't get back up and make a better life for yourself. Today, I am an undergrad in Psychology. I knew college would be in my future but I couldn't see past the 7th grade at the time. Don't allow your marriages, your schooling, or your failures to stop you from achieving a better life. If you wake up in the morning and you still have breath in your body, you can change your life circumstances. Just because you were born in it doesn't mean that you have to stay in it. Your life choices are up to you no matter what.

I had the worst marriage at 18. I thought that if I married him and loved him, he would love me. That was a huge disaster. When I turned 24, I didn't want to be in an uncommitted relationship, so I married again. I believed that he not being a Christian like me would make him turn his life around and he would become a God-fearing, loving man. Once again, that was another mistake that made me look at my life and say to myself, "Girl, you know this is not right. Something has to change." So, when I began to look at my life, I decided that I would not allow others in who were not going to help make me a better person. I was tired of allowing my life to be pulled down by others people's mess. My upbringing was messy enough; to pick up and carry other people's unsettled burdens was more than I could handle. I lost myself in all of the chaos. I couldn't even hear my own voice because I was always trying to make everyone else happy while I was dying inside. I finally got out of that marriage. I felt like a failure because I was supposed to be a Christian. I would help others in their relationships but couldn't help my own. But, I realize now that getting out and finding me was what I needed. I couldn't save the marriage, but I found myself. And today, I am one of the happiest women in the world. My life no longer waits on others. Instead, I learned to lean on and depend on God, and then make good decisions that will only add to my life and not pull or take away from it. Don't worry if you fail, just don't stay in that state. Get up and try again. And if that doesn't work, then get up and try again. Never give up! I am in such a state of peace within myself now that I can't even believe how great my life is. I wake up every morning with a smile on my face and it's because I learned that my failures don't define me.

Insecurities

As a teenager, I had a couple of friends, but for some reason that was not enough for me. I needed more. So I became a bodyguard for all that would pay me. That's how I made money and how I considered I acquired new friends. Oh, what a pity to feel so low about myself, but it was my way of survival, my way of feeling needed and most of all, wanted. So as time went on, I became more and more popular for my fighting skills and to tell you the truth, I loved every minute of it. I felt empowered and I felt like lots of people needed me. In all honesty, I really needed them, so one hand washed the other.

Then, instead of fighting all the time, I found myself mediating some of the problems. Instead of tearing people apart, I began bringing people together. I would have people apologizing to each other and everything—and I still got paid. It all worked for me. It's really funny how something so crazy was turned into something really good, because now I am an excellent counselor.

But it still didn't matter. I still had a need to feel the love that I was lacking, so I would find myself asking questions all the time concerning someone loving me. "Do you love me? Will you stay with me always? Will you always be my friend?" You know things along that line.

Once, when I worked at a fast food restaurant, I met a young sixteen-year-old guy by the name of Mike who worked there also. He was always very nice to me and never acted funny when he saw me come in to work. He actually acted pleased to see me, so I gravitated toward him because of his kindness. One day I asked Mike, "If you saw me later in life in the streets, would you always be nice to me? Would you still speak to me without any hesitation?"

I was thinking about all of those people who see you in the grocery store or the mall and won't stop because you are not important enough for them to talk to. I know everyone is not that way, because some people are really in a hurry, but you can generally tell whether you are wanted or not. Anyway, Mike told me yes, if he saw me anywhere he would always make time for me. It's funny that I even asked him that question at that time, because the business closed down suddenly and everyone from the job lost touch with one another. About eight or nine years later, who did I run into but Mike! He had become a police officer in our town and was patrolling the area of my father's place of residency. He recognized me and pulled over and said, "Hey, Michelle! Long time no see!" I turned around to this big cheesy smile.

I was so surprised because the question that I asked him years prior popped into my head, and that's when I realized that some people do keep their promises and everyone isn't bad. But Mike was still just as nice, or even nicer, then I remembered. Little things like that meant so much to me and I will always remember that.

Thanks Mike. You really don't know what you did for me by just being friendly.

As life progressed, I began to come into my looks, I began to feel pretty inside and out, and I had more clothes than I could fit into the closet. Sometimes you try to fill voids in your life by over doing it. After a while I realized I didn't need all those clothes. It was just a phase that I was going through when I thought that I would always have clothes, and the clothes would make me happy. When I finally realized what happiness was, I got rid of some of the clothes. My happiness was from within, my joy stemmed from God up above, and if I had God working on the inside, it would show on the outside. My joy or my deliverance had nothing to do with my clothes.

I had always thought that I needed a friend. All that has changed, too. I had become so popular, that I couldn't go anywhere without somebody recognizing me. People who I don't even know would come up to me and say, "I heard your CD" or "I saw your play." I have people who I've never met inquiring about me. Wow, life is funny! Who would have ever thought a little girl from downtown Kingston with hardly any friends in life, who had always been teased, put down, and abused, would ever amount to anything?

Hey, the Bible said it best—the first shall be last and the last shall be first. Thank God for the word. I truly feel blessed, and if you are one of those people, don't worry. Life gets better. Your latter days will be greater than your past. So get ready for your blessing and stretch out on faith and receive your miracle.

A Good Friend

I have a friend from childhood who stuck by me like glue. Her name is Sheila K. Swan, now known as Sheila K. Jones. She and I were like the worst of friends, and then after all the fighting that we did at the age of five and six we became the best of friends. I can honestly say that she was there through thick and thin.

We would get in trouble together and then we would play together. Our favorite thing was to go rollerskating every weekend. What I liked about Sheila was that when I was being punished for one thing or another that I did or didn't do and couldn't leave the porch, she would sit there with me for hours at a time.

Sheila was crazy. She had these little white mice as pets that I was terribly afraid of, but because she was my friend I wanted to try to like the nasty creatures (smile). One day one of them died and she wanted to have a funeral, so I stood in with her as she cried and buried her little white mouse outside in the back yard. I loved going to her house, but I was afraid of the mice. I kept hoping all of them would either run away or follow the one who went to mouse heaven.

That wouldn't have bothered me one bit, except that actually I never wanted to see Sheila sad or crying. She is one of the best and most honest people I know. She has real character. I always liked her because we never argued except for the few times when we were very little, and all that ceased. I've never had anyone in my life like her. She is like a fresh breath of air. She is like the wind that blows in on a hot desert day that says, "I'm here to cool you off." I like her because she loves to laugh, and because she is so sincere.

The same Sheila that I met as a child is the same Sheila that I know now. I always thank God for her. She reminds me of the relationship between Oprah Winfrey and her best friend, Gail.

They will never ever part, and I feel no matter what, Sheila will always be a part of my life. I know by her actions and in my heart that she loves me.

I could go on and on about my very best friend in the entire world. She was the person that held my hand when, at the age of thirteen, I ran through her back door and stopped breathing due to asthma and a very bad sinus. Her family rushed me to the hospital while my mom lay on the couch and wouldn't help me.

All I remember was lying on the floor with Sheila holding my head crying, "Please, God, don't let her die. No, God, don't let her die." No one had ever cried over me like that, and really meant it. Sheila was put in my life by God to know real love. She loved me when everyone teased me. She loved me when I was abused. She never left me when I got myself into trouble. As a matter of fact, she was often right there in it with me. To this day, we go to church together and talk on the phone almost every day. We are there for each other no matter what.

The only difference now is that we don't get in trouble. Now we try to keep our children out of trouble and lead them in the right direction. It's funny, we both have all girls. Who would ever have thought we'd have all girls? Yeah, we need prayer!

Anyway if anyone ever needed a friend, Sheila is the perfect candidate, because she is real, and you won't find anyone like her. I know I never will.

To my very best friend from childhood: I love you so much, and I always will. Thanks for always being there for me and never judging me. Thanks for laughing with me and not at me. I am so grateful to have you in my life and I thank God for you in my prayers all the time. Sheila, I can never say enough about you. We will be friends forever, for here and eternity. I love you girly—so, so, so much. Words will never express how much I appreciate you. My Bff! (Singing our song in my head right now. Good Morning Sheila, Good morning Missy ☺

Funny Things Do Happen

You want to hear something funny? I heard one of my friend's uncles had died, and I almost forgot about the funeral—actually I didn't forget because no one ever told me the day of the funeral. Ironically, I was on my way to Bible study one Wednesday night when I saw a crowd of people standing outside a church. As I passed by, I stopped and asked a woman if there was a church service or a revival or something going on. The woman informed me it was a funeral. I found out later that it was a wake service.

I figured since I knew the family I would go in and pay my respects. As I got out of the car, I realized that it was late in the hour and I didn't just want to go in looking for all the people that I haven't seen in a long time, so I kept my eyes focused on the casket that was straight ahead. As I walked slowly up to the front of the church, I felt all eyes on me. I thought maybe they were looking at me because I had on a black and white shirt that was fitted and a nice pair of slacks. My hair was long and flowing as I walked. I looked like I was going to the Grammy's, not to a wake.

As I continued to move forward, I was afraid to look at the casket, so I looked above it at that pretty material inside the inner part. I was a little afraid, but I wanted to support the family of the man who had died. I also wanted to see the people I haven't seen in a long time. As I reached the front, I knew that it was time to look down to see my friend's uncle. I braced myself and I looked, and my eyes got big when I saw a woman lying in the casket—and not only a woman, but a woman that I didn't even know. I stood there wondering who in the world she was.

Standing there in one spot, starring down in total shock, I noticed from the corner of my left eye a picture of the woman, but she didn't even look familiar. I pulled myself together and decided to at least look at the family, sure that I would know somebody because we are here in Kingston, my hometown. I didn't recognize one person! I stood still for a brief second and scanned the room for a ray of hope. Nope, not one. Now for me, that's strange, because I know everybody, and I mean everybody.

By now I was behind a woman who was giving the family her condolences. As she was passing through the line, I tried to think of what to say. What if they ask me a question? For the first time in my life I had an out-of-body experience, meaning I wished that I was out of my body.

I have never been a person who is at a loss for words, but I was drawing a blank. I overheard the woman in front of me say, "Oh, I'm so sorry. She was such a good woman." I thought, "That's it, that's it! What a perfect opportunity to speak!" I figured this would be a good time to allow my acting skills to kick in. I jumped right in and said, "Yes, she was a good woman." Then I proceeded to the next person in the front pew and said, "I am so sorry for your loss." For some crazy reason, I felt that because I was the center of attention at that moment, I had to use lots of expression when giving my words of comfort. I was thrown into a lion's den with nowhere to run. I felt kind of trapped.

Then someone asked me, "Who are you?" The funny thing was, they ask me if I was a part of the family of the funeral that I was supposed to be at. I said, "No, I am just here to show my support." I was in such shock that I didn't even remember who I was at that moment. I began making my way out to the front of the church and with great relief I saw a familiar face. I thought to myself that the deceased must not be from Kingston. I didn't ask any questions. I got out of there as fast as I possibly could, with a small smile of sympathy on my face to all that were in the hallway and outside the church. I found out later that it was a wake for a lady in our town and there were no familiar faces because of a lifetime of feud. The part of the family at the wake was from out of town. I never got to go to the young man's funeral that I thought I was supposed to be at. Now that's crazy, right? Smh I will never do that again.

Which brings me to another funeral I attended. It was for a dear family friend/cousin. Mom and I sat in the church for a while, being very attentive in the service and within a half hour I needed to use the bathroom. I got up and walked toward the bathroom and I saw one of my friend's brothers shaking his head. I wondered what was going on, but I just kept on walking into the bathroom.

I opened the door and to my surprise, there was a lady standing over the sink with a ponytail sticking up on top of her head with a big green trash bag full of dirty clothes. She bent down and started pulling more dirty clothes out of the bag and washing them by hand in the sink. I tried to walk past her to use the bathroom and as I looked up, I saw she had clothes hanging on the bathroom door. She said, "Oh, you can go ahead and use the toilet. Don't worry about those clothes. The door will still shut."

I couldn't believe it; she was washing and hanging clothes out at the funeral instead of being out in the service for her aunt. I thought that was the funniest thing that I had seen in a very long time. Well, maybe in all of my time. A couple of people came up and just looked at her while she continued on washing clothes. I walked out of that bathroom and laughed through the whole funeral. I couldn't seem to pull myself together. Now that was hilarious.

CHAPTER 10

He Adored Me

I remember someone who adored me, he laughed at everything that I did and said and we were never without conversation. His given name was Raymond, and he was my brother Snooky.

We were very close. Our birthdays were four days apart, mine August 12 and his August 16. Sometimes we just don't understand the process of death, and honestly, I don't think that we ever will. But one thing is for sure: I really did appreciate the time that we spent together, because I had nothing but love for him and I always will. I often wonder to myself what it would be like now if he were still alive. I still have a longing for him, and sometimes losing him still hurts. When you had someone to love you the way that he loved me, it feels like a double loss.

My brother and I had a strong connection. He was always looking out for me and I would do the same for him. Once when we were sitting on the bed while my mom folded laundry, I suddenly had an open vision. I saw the metal blind falling from the window, hitting my brother and leaving him with a bloody slice across his face. It shocked me for a second, because it seemed so real. I looked at him as he smiled at me, then I noticed that the blind was really about to fall. I jumped across the bed and lay over his body so he wouldn't get cut. The blind fell and cut me above my eye.

I didn't realize what had just happened, and neither did my brother. We just looked at each other in disbelief. I ended up with a few stitches on my eyebrow. Every stitch was worth it. I will never regret that moment for as long as I live. I don't know if my mom knew what actually transpired at that moment, but I always felt like my brother's little hero, whether my mom knew I was saving my brother's face or not. I told my brother why I did what I did, but I felt he already knew because of our connection. I can't really explain it, but we had something so special that it was beyond words. His blood for mine. I would do it again, all because I love him.

Don't Lie to Your Children about Death!

The day Snooky died, my younger brother and I were lying in the bed when my father came in and told us that he had passed.

I clearly remember Jay crying so loud in my ear that I rolled over and told him to shut up. Like that was going to stop a five-year old from crying! I shouldn't have said that though, because maybe they had a special relationship, too. But being so young at that time, I didn't understand what was happening.

I do remember being very angry that Snooky was gone.

I never cried. I just stayed angry all the time, until one night my father took us outside and said, "Your brother will always be with you. Look, there. He is right there."

"Where?" I asked.

"Do you see that star right there?" he replied.

I said yes, because it was the biggest star that I had ever seen.

Dad said, "Well, that's him. So anytime you want to see Snooky, just look up and he is there."

And I believed him. Every night I would try to find the star and talk to it, Then there were nights when the star didn't come out and I figured he just didn't want to play or he was busy helping God. It didn't bother me when he couldn't come out to play. This may sound strange, but I kept that concept in my head until I was thirteen years old.

I continued to bond with my brother as I stared into the night sky. I felt this warm connection, such as when I had to walk in the dark to the store, he was with me. Finally, one day in school we began to study the universe and all that comes with it. That's right, we began to study stars and to my surprise the person that I was having all these encounters with was the North Star. My teacher and I got into a debate about the star. After a good long talking to and lots of books for proof, I began to believe her. I knew that she was telling the truth.

I came home that day very confused, though. Later on that night, lo and behold, the North Star came out and I began to cry.

I felt like I had been lied to. At that moment, I began to grieve. I cried like a baby for days upon days. I was severely depressed, because now I didn't know where my brother really was. He was not my shining star anymore. Now what was I supposed to do? I was angry at my parents for lying to me. I know they only did what they thought was best for us at the time, but I don't know if they understood how it would affect me.

I am such a thinker, and I meditate very hard on things. Their lie took its toll on me as a child and given all that I was going through, it just added fuel to my fire. I still had no sound council, no one to console me or hold me to let me know that all was going to be well. Finally I made it over that strong hurdle but it wasn't easy. I realized after a long time that it was God who was with me all the time, because His Word says that He would never leave me nor forsake me. After a while I came to the realization that my brother was all right—and so was I.

P.S. to Snooky: We will meet again one day in heaven, and you will always be a star in my eyes because only stars rest in the sky.

How a child can be molested right in front of you.

Do you know who is holding your baby? At first, it's all innocent because babies have that smell that makes you want to kiss them. He kisses her soft lips, and then as she gets older she learns how to squirm. Now she's in his lap and his erection is being hidden by her pampered bottom. As she gets a little older, you hear those familiar words, "Where's my little girl?" And she runs to him with open arms. He lifts her up and gets a peek under her little skirt as he slides her down his chest and holds her near his private parts. The hugs become more intense as she jumps all over him. He begins to release a soil that's undetectable by Mom because her first thoughts are, "Boy, he sure loves this baby." Before you know it, time has allowed her to feel good every time Uncle comes over. She continues to run to him every time she sees him, until one day he just cannot control himself. He now lays her back and tells her, "This won't hurt. Uncle loves you, ok." He may or may not penetrate her at that moment depending on what kind of man he is. If he is violent, May God have mercy on his soul, he will pierce her soul and there will be screams of intensity that will tear her apart, or he will be gentle and stroke the parts of her that stimulate him or her. Guilt hits him as he's consumed with the quench of his thirst being fulfilled. How can he experience two powerful feelings at one time? He backs off as she cries and reaches for him with her limp body. Then he hugs her, kisses her, rocks her, lays his head on her chest and says, "Shhhhhh. Shhhhh. Don't cry. I'm here. Everything is going to be alright." This vicious cycle continues to happen and then you see two of your children on Uncle's lap. And the first thing that mom says is, "Boy, does Uncle love the children." Now those children begin fighting for Uncle's attention, while another child seems quiet and observant. How does he get away with it? Because when he gets to your home you ask, "Can you watch the kids as I run to the store, or the doctor's appointment, or just run some errands?" Now this person has total access to your children. Until one day he's gotten sloppy and you find out that your child has now been touched for years. How could a Mom or Dad not have known? A parent's guilty questions: "How could I not have known? How could this happen? How do I call the cops on my brother or family member, my son, my lover? How?" A parent holds their head in shame with tears of not protecting their children. Mom says, "Where do I go from here? How do I protect my children from anyone I love now because my trust for all has been shattered?" God, help the mother about whom everyone is saying, "She should have known." People need to know that some mothers were just side swiped. They never saw it coming. In life, don't be so quick to judge because as the Bible says, "Judge not lest ye be judge by the same measure." Matthew 7:1-2. KJV Meaning: it could happen to you. So, be careful how you deal with people who have experienced such harshness. Watch your children closely.

CHAPTER 11

I Did It for Love's Sake

Nobody ever told me that I would have to raise three children on my own, but for the love of my beautiful ones, I did it. I had my first child at the age of eighteen—maybe for the wrong reasons, but it fulfilled my need. I was quite loveless and I wanted to have something to love.

I was always full of love but it seemed like no real love was being returned to me. So I had my first daughter. It was a beautiful thing because she looked at me with those big baby brown eyes and smiled, and I felt I had just beheld love. For the first time in my life I began to experience real love. Whenever she cried, I ran to her rescue because I didn't want my baby to hurt the way that I was hurting. I never wanted her to cry because of me. When she was hungry I fed her until she was stuffed. There would never be a hungry day in that child's life.

I wanted her to be so close to me that I carried her on my hip for the first two years. The only reason I put her down was because I was pregnant with my next little love, J'nai. And a couple years later I was on number three and her name is Jahon. I loved my babies. I began craving a baby at the age of fifteen. I knew what I wanted even though it came with a high cost.

I needed something in my life to love and I needed it quickly. Were there ever times that I wanted to quit? Yes. But I made these three little decisions and it was my responsibility to care for them the best that I knew how. I knew even though my emotional state was rocky, I was equipped to handle this challenge. Having children was not the easiest. There were days when we had no food, and I breast fed my children beyond the time that I probably should have, but there was nothing too good for my babies.

There were times when I had no money for clothes for my

children and I would go to the Salvation Army red box and take the donations on the outside. Sometimes I would even climb inside to try to get the best clothes that I could for them. I am not proud to say that, but that's how I was living and I did what I had to do to survive.

And believe me, it was a struggle to survive. My children's father and I split up and I was left with no child support and all of the responsibility that comes with raising children. I wanted love so that it all became so overwhelming, what was I to do?

I was standing in lines to receive food from pantries. I had to go to a place called Birthright to get cribs for my children. It seemed all I could do just to keep a smile on my face that said "all is well." At one point I had a house full of furniture from Rent-A-Center, and the bill was not being paid because of the finances with my ex. I had a 10-piece sectional and bedroom sets for the kids and me. One day they came in and took all of their belongings back from me, and I was left with an empty living room and no bedroom sets. But they did leave one thing—the mattress—and I began to cry uncontrollably. I didn't cry because they took everything from me, I cried because they left the mattress, and I was grateful to just have something to sleep on so my babies and I would not have to sleep on the floor. It was more to me than just a mattress; it was for the love of my children.

It's Not that Easy Raising Kids

Nobody ever told me that it would be easy raising kids. There were some stories that were told to me and some TV shows that I watched that made me believe that there was more to raising children than what I knew. Because I am a hopeless romantic, I loved to watch TV shows like Leave It to Beaver, The Brady Bunch and little short series that enhanced the family. But for some reason—maybe you can help me with this—it wasn't that way in my home! Every time I watched TV, I saw the happy family, like the man of the house playing ball with his son, the mother in the kitchen teaching her daughters how to cook, the grandmother in the living room knitting, and the grandpa out in the garage fixing whatever was broken. And let's not forget the music that comes on TV to complete the picture perfect home.

My family was nothing at all like that. I never heard any violins playing when I was feeding my kids or when I was talking to them to correct them in their wrong doings. Maybe just having enough food for that day was my song—the little song "thank you, Lord" that rang in my heart. And the only orchestra that played at dinner time was the children banging their spoons and bowls on the table wanting their food in a hurry. If I had to rewrite a script for a movie, it would be entitled "This Is the Way It Really Is."

Sleepless Nights

One night as I waited up for my daughter, Savanna, I receive a phone call. She's told me that my two sisters were fighting in the car on the highway. Even before all this occurred, I felt in my spirit that something was going to happen. I was with them earlier that night and I told them before we separated, "Don't let the devil come in." We had just left a church service that was on fire—it was awesome. All of my sisters and my niece in one place at one time with me at church, now that was a miracle in itself! So when we left that night, I rode home with a friend and my sisters and daughters and another friend rode home together in my truck.

When I got home I received the phone call, and I began to pray. As parents we have built-in radar and it has different levels of alert. I knew that something was wrong, but I still had a sense of peace that she would eventually come home. I prayed with my youngest daughter that God would cover everyone in the vehicle and keep them safe.

Even though I had a sense of peace, it was 3:18 in the morning, and I decided to go look for Savanna. There was no answer when I called and no sign of them as I drove up and down the town looking for my vehicle. I went to all of my sisters' familiar places that they could or would be, but there was no sign of them. The last time that I heard from my daughter was at 11:30 p.m. and they had been halfway home then when the fight occurred. I then found out that my sister, Tykey, was home, and she said that my other sister went back out onto the highway looking for her wallet that Tykey had thrown out the window during the fight. By then,

I'd gone past worrying and was straight angry.

I came back home and I got back on my knees. I didn't stay down there long; all I ask God to do was bring my baby home soon, please. As I was praying I heard a car beep outside, so instantly I ran to the door to see who it was. It wasn't them. Being a parent is not an easy job when you are sitting there wishing and praying that every car or every little noise hear is your child. Finally, after praying again, I began to get very sleepy. I almost felt guilty not feeling so worried anymore. I thanked God that the door was locked, because with my luck, she would walk in and catch me knocked out and have the thought in her head that I wasn't worried about her. Yeah, right!

About an hour later, I heard the door, and then I heard a knock. I knew it was Savanna because as parents we know all about the little things that in times like this mean so much. For instance, if it had been a bang at the door I would have known that might mean trouble, like the police coming to render some bad news or something. Instead it was that familiar screen door swing and that soft pleasant knock that said, "Mommy, it's me. Could you let me in?"

In a split second I ran to the door. I didn't even ask who it was because in my heart I already knew. It was now 5:35 in the morning, and I wasn't used to my daughter ever coming home after midnight or one, and that was from the prom. As I opened the door, I saw Savanna standing there between my sister and her friend. I looked her up and down for a tenth of a second to make sure that she was all right. To the left was my sister Christine. Her eyes looked pretty big and her mouth was tightly shut. I must have had a look on my face that scared them all, because they all looked at me as if to say, "There is no explaining this one."

I motioned to Savanna and her friend, Destiny, with my thumb, and it said "get in this house now." My balled up fist and my one thumb said it all. With the same fist, I gave Christine a small wave and shut the door. The only voices I heard were Savanna telling Christine goodnight and her reply of goodbye. My hand did all the speaking that night because my lips were shut so tight; no words could have been spoken. Savanna and Destiny went straight to bed without a peep.

I locked the door and came back into the living room and lay on the couch with an enormous sense of relief. I thanked God with a big sigh. Oh, how wonderful to feel free from the inner tension!

Despite the sense of peace, something began to happen, and in a matter of moments, all the "what ifs…?" arose. Every time I tried to close my eyes I saw my sisters fighting on the road, and felt how scared everyone must have been because of their selfishness. I kept seeing all the bad things that could have happened. How dare they put my daughter's life in danger! I got down right mad. I couldn't wait until later on that day, because I had a thing or two to tell them. Given the emotional roller coaster that I had been on, I prayed one more time for guidance on how to deal with the situation.

I wonder if my mom ever sat up for me like this. If so, I'm so sorry.

Christmas Memories

One Christmas morning I woke up extra early, sat on the steps, looked at the tree, and said a little prayer to Santa Claus asking him to bring me a doll with long hair. I was so excited just thinking about what I was going to get! My mom walked by and I asked her, "Did I get anything, Mommy?" She said, "No." I thought she was just saying that because it wasn't actually time to open up the presents. I went upstairs and prayed even harder to Santa. "Please, Santa. I promise that I will be good from now on. I won't do anything bad anymore from now on." I then went to sleep hoping that there would be something for me under the tree. I woke up and ran down the stairs and straight to the tree where my brother and sisters were opening up all of their presents. My brother had the Hess truck in his hand and was reaching for the next present with his name on it. My three little sisters had all kinds of things open and were still grabbing for their next presents. I began to look for something with my name on it. I moved all of the unopened presents out of the way as I continued to look for something with my name on it. Still nothing. I thought Mom and Dad were playing a trick on me, so I played along with them and waited for about 5 minutes. After watching my little sisters and brother with happy faces, I realized that there was nothing under the tree for me. I stood there as the tears ran down my face. I couldn't believe it! Mom wasn't kidding. I really didn't get anything. As the tears rolled down my face, my brother and sisters never even noticed that I didn't get anything; they were so happy with their own gifts. I felt like an outsider looking in. I walked back over to the steps and sat down and watched them. They were all so happy. Mom and Dad never looked at me nor said a word to me. I was hoping that the tears would cause them to feel guilty enough to find something for me; anything would have done. But, still nothing. I left that unhappy scene of the perfect family Christmas without me, went up to my room and cried myself to sleep. I felt unwanted. As a child, I didn't understand why I hadn't received anything. It made me think that maybe I was a bad child. As I grew into a woman, I carried that grief into my adult life. It caused me to never have a passion for Christmas. At that time, I didn't understand that Christmas was about the life of Christ. When I had children, I always went out of my way to make sure that they had a decent Christmas and learned its real meaning. Every year that I set up a tree for my children, I always watched them open their presents with joy. But, after they opened their presents and went to their rooms, I always sat and cried because I was hurt. I realized that I never got over the pain of that one Christmas.

It's years later and my life is wonderful right now; but, as I am writing this passage, I still feel hurt because no child should ever feel left out or unwanted. I really never understood what I could have done so bad that made my parents leave me feeling that way. But today, I am a better person because of that experience. I am a giver because I never received. I work with children and I always love to give them the things I never received. It feels good to do that for someone who feels like there is no hope. I also know now that favoring one child over the other is never good for sibling relationships. If you are a parent and this is something that you are doing or have done, it's never too late to turn it around. If you did this or something like this, you can be the bigger person and say, "I am sorry that I hurt you." You can make things right. "I'm sorry" goes a long way when you really mean it. It changes the hard heart of the person who is harboring uneasy feelings toward you. Also, if this is something you've found yourself doing, change your ways immediately because you don't want your child to carry it into adulthood. This is something that could literally ruin not only their lives but even their children's lives due to an unsettled sense of loss.

What Is Life Really About?

Life is about sacrifices
Life is about sufferings
Life is about enjoyment
Life is about happiness
Life is full of sorrow
Life is full of wisdom
Life is full of knowledge
Life is full of greatness
Life is full of kindness
Life is full of hatred
Life is honored with encouragement
Life is dishonored with discouragement
Life is sometimes cruel
Life is sometimes sweet
Life is sometimes gracious
Life is often greedy
Life is always full
Life is always sometime-me
Life is always about something
Life is life
If we figured out life
There wouldn't be a need to live

Because life is a never ending story
Just live because life lives on

.

CHAPTER 12

My Mother, My Friend

For a long time I did not forgive my mother for all of the craziness I suffered growing up in our home. But as I grew up and learned a little about life myself, I began to see why she was the way that she was. And it made it a little easier for me to forgive her. Eventually, my mother and I began going to church together and to bond like never before. All I really ever wanted was to be wanted and be her friend.

My mother was the strongest woman that I knew in my entire life. As I was growing up, I never saw my mother cry. She was like Wonder Woman to me, and maybe that's the reason I am as strong as I am today. One day we were in church and the pastor called her up for prayer, hugged her, and said, "You have been carrying lots of hurt and God hears your prayers and he is answering them just for you."

I was standing behind my mother as the words went forth and then out of the clear blue, I watched my mother cover her face and the pastor tell her, "It's okay. It's okay to cry." The tears began to stream down my mother's face and I did all I could do not to break down and cry with her. I couldn't believe my mother was crying; she had feelings. At that moment I realized that my mother was a wounded soul and she didn't know how to release in front of people. She cried so hard that I eventually broke down and cried, too.

The pastor said to her, "God sees you crying late at night, when no one is watching," and my mother cried even more. The pastor hugged her and told her that she is loved and that God does care about her and what she was going through. At that moment, I knew in my heart that my mother was no different from me or anyone else I knew. She had a heart and she had feelings and her feelings did hurt her just like mine did. My mother held things inside and always put on a smile like nothing ever bothered her.

I began to know that she needed love too.

I became what I thought I would never be to my mother—a friend. She needed a true friend in her life and I knew that I could be just that. I believe that she wanted the same from me because she couldn't be there for me in the way that she wanted to be as I grew up. When I was younger, I always wanted to hug my mother. When I saw her on the couch, I would run up and put my arms around her and she would push me away.

I don't remember my mother saying she loved me while I was growing up—not one time. After we became friends, we were at another church service one night and I was preaching. God had me have everyone to go around and hug each other and tell the person that you loved them. As I walked around the church hugging people, I got to my mother and I hugged her and not really thinking, I said, "I love you."

It was quick and I was getting ready to move on to the next person, but as I tried to pull away, my mother tugged on me and would not let me go. I stayed just a little while longer with the microphone in my hand still leading people into telling others that they love them. My mother kept holding on. Almost as though she had turned into a little child, she began holding me and rocking back and forth, giving a little child-like laugh while she was in my arms.

For the first time ever, I heard the words from my mother that I was longing to hear since I was a child. She said, "I love you, Missy." I was shocked because she said it as she was still holding me tight and she not only said it once, but she said it again and called my name.

I felt the connection between us so strongly, I wondered, "Oh, my goodness, what is God up to? What is he doing in my life? Is he fulfilling my dreams for the first time in this friendship?" Yeah, he was, and it felt so, so good. When she finally let go, I had tears in my eyes and she had a big smile on her face like, "There I finally did it, and it wasn't hard after all."

That was one month before my mother died. We were the best of buddies. Where I went, she went. We were like Tom and Jerry—inseparable. She not only became my best friend she became my support and my biggest fan in life. She promoted me to all that she knew and to them that she didn't know. After my mother's death, my aunt told me that all she talked about was me and how well I was doing and how proud she was of me.

One day I had taken my mother out grocery shopping and bought her some food. As she stood in the door with her bags when I dropped her off back at the house, she turned around and said, "Thank you, Missy," with a look I had never seen before. I was looking at her like, "Mom, what is happening here?" When she said it, it went all through me like lightning. A week after that she was gone. I believe that she wanted me to know that she loved me and that she appreciated everything I did for her. Now she is at ease in her spirit when it comes to me, because she truly made her peace. Not only did I forgive her, but she did the hardest thing a person could do, she forgave herself.

Mom, just a little note to you:
I always loved you even when I
Was mad, all I ever wanted was for
You to want me and to be proud of me.
That was my lifetime dream,
And I just want to say thank you
Because you made all of my dreams
Come true, just by being there for me
And loving me, and not only loving me
But Mom, you learned to love yourself

Mom Died

In the latter days of life with Mom, she was always the one around to take care of Dad when he was sick. Those cigarettes sure did a number on my dad's health. He wasn't that bad off when Mom was alive, but if he needed anything she was always there. Mom did lots of things for all of us as life progressed. She had sugar diabetes and she took insulin everyday. She did her best to walk and eat right for her health's sake. She seemed healthy, beyond a few colds or maybe a little bit of vertigo.

A month before anything happen to my mother, I had a dream that she and I were sitting at a little white table in her house, just a chatting away. I leaned down just for a second to grab something out of my bag and when I looked back up, Mom had fallen to the floor with a heart attack. The dream had troubled me, because I am a dreamer and lots of my dreams come true. This dream was strong and I felt like it had real meaning.

The next day I told my sister Christine about the dream, including how real it seemed. She said, "What if we are all so worried that it's Daddy and it's really Mommy." As the month passed, Christine began doing all of these extra nice things for Mom. She got her a pedicure and hung out with her and me real close, going shopping and anything else that she could do to make Mom happy. Christine got Mom's hair done for her, and she was in her glory.

One day Chris and I were sitting in our mother's bedroom talking as sisters do, and I decided to pop my head out and see what Mom was doing. She was talking to her boyfriend, which didn't surprise me. What did startle me was the way she was talking to him and the way that she looked as she spoke these words of wisdom and instruction. I called to Christine to come and look at Mommy. We both just stared in disbelief. She looked ten or fifteen years younger, and she was speaking big words with no hesitation.

My mom she wasn't anywhere near what we were hearing in her vocabulary. She was a smart woman, but she was talking like a professor. That was very weird.

Later on that month, Mom bought a swimming pool for the grandchildren. She kept calling Christine to tell her about the pool and she couldn't reach her. She and Christine had finally bonded and mended their feelings of uneasiness. It was nice to see them so happy together. Chris always felt that Mom didn't care for her as much because she was Daddy's favorite girl—Daddy's little Indian—and she told Dad everything about Mom—and I mean everything. Mom tried to be sneaky sometimes, and if he wanted to know, all he had to do was ask Chris. If Dad was going out the front door, Mom's boyfriend would be coming in the back door and Christine would make it her business to run and tell Daddy before he made it to the car.

Anyway, Mom kept calling me, still trying to find Chris to tell her about the pool. Mom told me that day she had reached her sister, who she hadn't spoken to in over a year. She hadn't been able to find her because she moved somewhere in North Carolina with no phone contact. Mom was so happy. She said they talked for hours. Later on, I found Christine and she came right past my mother's house where I stood at the bottom of the steps. She told my mom that she had to take care of something but would be right back.

I walked with Christine over to Carmine's and when I returned to my mother later, she was standing on the porch. She seemed a little aggravated that she never got to show Christine the swimming pool. It was alright, though, because mom started talking about her sister again and she got happy.

That night, I called Mom to check on her as I always did with both my parents. She sounded frantic. She was upset about the neighbors who where outside arguing and fighting. She told me on the telephone that she wanted to move. I told her I would be there early in the morning to pick her up and take her out to look for a new place. Mom said once again, "I am out of here." I just let her talk because she was very upset. We finally said goodnight and I fell asleep.

About four hours later, I receive a phone call. It must have been about two in the morning. I heard Christine say, "I am on my way to Mommy's house. I see an ambulance down there, I feel something in my heart and it doesn't feel right. I'll call you right back." She must have run down there because within two minutes she called me back, asking, "What kind of medicine does Mommy take?"

I told her insulin, and she told the EMTs. They kept asking questions and she in turn kept asking me. They ask if she had asthma, I told her no. I heard my mother in the background saying, "Help! Help." Christine said Mom was holding her throat. My sister was getting really upset and I told her to calm down.

The screams in the background from my mother got more and more intense, "Help, please help!" My heart dropped. My sister continued, "You have to see Mommy! Something is not right!"

All of a sudden, there was a loud thump. It was so loud that I heard it through the phone. "Oh my God! Mommy just passed out! Christine reported. Within a matter of moments, she jumped back into consciousness, begging again for help. Christine said Mom kept reaching for her for help. My sister was crying and asking, "What can I do for you, Mommy? How can I help you? Please tell me." Mom's cries for help began to sound like her lungs were filling up with something, like a gurgle.

It seemed like a long time, but actually it happened so fast, we were all in shock. I told my sister that I was on my way. I called my other sister, Valerie, and we caught a ride uptown with a police officer. The back of that police car made me feel like I was going to die. It had no air, no door handles, nothing at all, and the only thing in front of me was a cage. I began to feel sick. It seemed like the longest ride that I ever took in my life.

When we finally got there, my brother Jay was holding Christine in his arms and she was crying like she was having a breakdown. She was shaking and pointing, telling me to go see Mommy. I was scared. Valerie and I walked into the hallway and there stood my dad just watching them work on her. I saw my mother's feet shaking; she was seizing. I never liked seizures. I couldn't even stand to watch, it bothered me so much, My mom was on the floor shaking all over, her body breaking down on her.

I came back outside and Christine asked, "Did you see her?"

"I can't look," I replied.

"You have to see her," she insisted.

I went around the back of the house and I began to pray, "Mommy, if you can hear me, you get back here. Don't leave!"

But the words felt empty. I was so scared to walk in and see her. My mom and I were so close, I didn't want to see her in any pain. It hurt me that she was suffering. I finally got myself together from being scared out of my wits and walked in through the back door. She was still shaking a little bit, but the seizure calmed down until it finally stopped. They had a tube down her throat that was pulling up a thick light brown fluid that was flowing very fast. Her eyes were closed and she lay still.

Everyone now entered the house. As we all stood there

watching my mother on the floor, her blood pressure dropped rapidly and her heart rate was very slow. The next thing I knew, they started pumping her chest. They kept pumping and pumping until I saw a line going across the screen. Mom had flat-lined, but they continue to pump and pump.

I ran out the back door, saying, "Mommy, please come back! Jesus help us, please!" I ran straight to my pastor's house and knocked and knocked until she came to the door. "I think my mother is dead," I told her. "I don't think that she is coming back! I don't think that she is coming back!"

We stood there for a few moments and the ambulance came around the corner right past my pastor's house. We could see right through the ambulance window that they were still pumping her chest. I said, "See, Pastor, she is not coming back!"

We all ended up at the hospital with everyone all upset. I was calm for everyone else, but still a little shaken and upset about how my mother sounded during her ordeal. They worked and worked on Mom until they couldn't do any more. They came out of the room a hour and a half later and pronounced her dead.

I had heard a loud scream from inside the hospital. It was my baby sister, Tykey. I was outside with Sheila and a few others and we had all run in and they told us all that Mom was gone. I was numb. I was afraid to go in and view her. I couldn't cry. My pastor told me that I really should go in and see Mom. It took me a good while before I could look at her. Out of fear, I stood by the doorway viewing her from there.

Finally my pastor held my hand and walked me over to see her. She looked pretty as always, but she had blood coming out of her nostrils from the tubes that they put up her nose. I couldn't stay long. My sister Christine was rubbing her and all that. I reached over and touched her arm with three of my fingers. I couldn't do it, and I had to leave the room. I was filled with so much fear that after leaving the hospital, I couldn't even go home. Valerie and I went to her house and sat outside the door.

It was about six in the morning when we had left for the hospital. It's really funny how fast word spreads around town. As we were sitting there, a car came zooming up next to mine and the man leaned over and asked, "Is it true about Mrs. Cook? Is it true that she passed on?" Valerie and I said yes. We were so surprised.

It had been less than ten minutes since we'd left the hospital.

I went and stayed at my friend Sheila's house. I couldn't go home; I was afraid of my own house. I wasn't used to anyone dying who was so close to me. I thought that something was going to happen. I was really bugging out, like Mom was going to come and say something to me or something. After five days, my kids and I went home. Still afraid, we tried to lay down to rest. It was the night before the funeral. I couldn't bring myself to go to the funeral home to get her dressed or help do her hair.

That night my daughter, J'nai, lay on the floor next to me on the couch. She said, "Mommy, I feel scared." I said, "So do I, Honey," and we both lay there holding each other's hand for comfort. I began dosing off because I had not slept in all the day's since she passed.

I took half of a muscle relaxant on the fourth day which helped me a bit. By the fifth day I was ready for rest, but I was worried about what Mom was going to look like at the funeral tomorrow and how was I going to handle seeing her again.

I was so upset and uptight that I had to pray and pray hard.

Something happened that changed me as I lie there on the couch.

I saw something that looked like my mother, but in a spirit form.

She came and lay over J'nai and she said to me, "You can rest now.

I have J'nai." Within a matter of moments, I was sleep.

When I woke up the next morning I felt good and peaceful. I told J'nai I felt good. She said she did, too, and that she didn't know if she was dreaming, but Grandma had come to see her.

"She did come," I assured her. "I saw her, but I wanted to make sure that I wasn't bugging out."

A few hours later, we were at the funeral. I wasn't afraid anymore. I walked straight up to the casket and looked at my mother. What made me do that, I don't know. What took all that fear away? I know it was God.

The funeral was beautiful and I could not have asked for anything better. My family sang the song "Mama" by Boy'z to Men. It came out beautifully. My daughter, Jahon, sang so lovely. It was not like a funeral, but more like a musical tribute for my mother. She had so many flowers at the service. There were so many people at the funeral that there wasn't enough room for them, and we held it at a very large church. Cars were parked a mile down the road.

When we finally got to the burial ground, we said our goodbyes. As they were saying the last words, a sudden wind came and blew through us. We all just looked at each other and we all knew that it was our mom. We knew that she was okay; she must have just received her wings. We all proceeded back to the church to eat. It didn't feel like we were at a funeral; it felt very peaceful.

I was very good to my mother, I had never mistreated her and I always looked out for her in any way I could. Eventually I cried, but I cried because I missed her, and it's good to say that I have no regrets in my mother's death.

I love you, Mom.

Apple Butter

Sometimes I just sit around and converse with my family and we laugh and joke about things. At first we didn't talk about her much after her death, and I asked myself if it was wrong not to speak about her as much as we spoke about others. We hadn't forgotten her, but it hurt to lose Mom so suddenly. It's kind of like a deep hole inside of my heart, almost like a burning feeling. I guess that's what happens when you miss someone so much.

Apple butter was my mom's and my favorite. We would be in the grocery store and we would open up our own separate jars and begin to eat it as we shopped. Oh, it tastes so good! It was the highlight of our shopping trip every time. Every since Mom died, I haven't eaten apple butter, let alone bought it. Maybe I should try buying it and eating it in her memory and for the sake of my taste buds. Maybe it will help me fight through the grief of Mom being gone. Yeah, maybe I will do just that.

CHAPTER 13

Saying Goodbye to Dad

Nobody ever told me that when I watched my father go into respiratory arrest that I would literally go into shock. I mean, I stood and watched them stick a tube down his throat, and while he was awake. It was the scariest thing that I have ever seen in my life. I stood with my whole family in horror as we watched my dad's body practically leaping up and down on the hospital bed. I saw a tear run down his face. I didn't know if he was crying or if it was a tear from being gagged by the support tube.

Sometimes I wonder why I have to see so much. This one really hurt me. They had his arms and body strapped down to the bed as they kept trying to sedate him. For some reason, the sedation wasn't working. As I stood and watched, I felt as though I were floating, like I just couldn't pull myself together even if I tried. It felt like an out-of-body experience. I fell into a chair scared out of my wits, and I heard people talking around me but I couldn't respond.

I walked around for three days in this state. On the third day, I woke up and I didn't want to get dressed or do anything. After being up about ten minutes, I heard a voice say to me, "I rose up on the third day and so will he."

All of a sudden I got a burst of energy from out of nowhere and I went down to the hospital. As I was heading toward my dad's room in the ICU, I heard someone hollering and as I got closer I saw my father through his window sitting straight up in bed with his tube in his hand hollering, "Hey, hey."

I didn't even go into his room. I immediately ran and got the nurse. I didn't know what to feel. I felt like I was going through a series of events because I was totally scared. The nurses ran into the room, while I stood in the hall in total fright. The nurse came back into the hallway and ask me how it happened. She had the nerve to ask me if I pulled the plug out of his mouth, because his hands were strapped. I looked at her like she was crazy. Now why would I do a thing like that? I was scared and upset. I feel like his angels came in the room, and they did it. Ha, ha!

Later on that evening, he was sitting up eating, laughing and talking. He came out of the ICU the very next day and out of the hospital within the next few days. After a few days of being home, he told me that he had died and it was very peaceful. He never even remembered any of the traumas that he experienced. He said that his journey was quiet. He went looking for my mom and his son, and for his family. He said that he had seen no one, and God told him that he had to go back, that it wasn't his time yet, and that He had some things that He had to show him.

He seemed to be hallucinating for a while—but then again was he? When you have a near death experience, who's to say what's real and what's not. I tell you one thing: he saw something, because he changed. He said that he wasn't afraid to die anymore and when it was his time to go that he would be okay, that he would be ready. That helped me to let go and leave it to God. Sometimes we try to play God, and we know it never really works. I am not God and I learned that His perfect will has to be done regardless to what I feel or even think. God is bigger than me—and that's that.

Have You Ever Had to Pull the Plug?

It happened to my family. I never knew that I would be in that position. When my mother died there was no choice, she just had a massive heart attack and she was gone, with no if ands or butts about it. My father, though, was rushed to the hospital on September 13, of 2004 at about 12 p.m. and placed on life support for the second time because he stopped breathing due to emphysema.

I was out of town. One of the worst things that can happen to you is wanting to get somewhere in a hurry but you can't due to traffic. Even if you could go 100 miles an hour, you wouldn't get there quick anyway, because no matter how fast you go, time seems to stand still when you hear something that awful about your loved one.

While on the phone, I could hear my sister saying, "Get here, because this time it is the worst that I've ever seen him." I had never heard my sister cry on the phone. Actually, both my sisters were crying. Out of all the times that my father was hospitalized, this time we were dealing with a dead man being revived by a machine. If my father was going to die, I wanted to be with him. I tried to pray as much as I could. This was a time that my faith was being put to the test. You always tell others to pray when things occur, but now it was my turn to receive what I had told others. Believe me, it was hard, but I can tell you this much, God understood my groaning and I believe He took them into consideration. God, I just want to say thank you.

When I finally arrived in the emergency room, my father was sedated and fully unaware of his surroundings and stayed that way for about two weeks. The doctors tried to take him off the respirator after about a week but he struggled so hard he just couldn't make it without the machine. He had to be put back on life support and that scratched his throat and bruised his esophagus. The doctors gave our family an alternative. They said that our father was very unlikely to make it this time, and if he did by some unknown miracle, he would have no quality of life. He would probably need a tracheotomy tube placed in his throat.

As we faced all of this, they told us that he would have to be taken off the respirator on that Thursday, September 23rd. We had to decide whether, if he couldn't breathe on his own, he should have the surgery to put in trachea tube. We didn't want him to let him go, but what kind of life would that be for him? So we all tried to prepare ourselves for that day. It was so weird going through the anticipation that on Thursday my father might live or he might die. I never thought I would be a part of a decision that could mean the end of life for another person. A part of me was so afraid that I was taking a human life away. What if I was killing him? I couldn't deal with that.

It was the hardest thing I ever suffered through. I thought that I was prepared for all of this because my father had been sick for a very long time, Along with my family, I saw the ends and the outs of his suffering, but still, letting go of someone you love is never easy. "This is not a job for me," I thought. "This job is too big for me and I can't handle it." I looked up to God and asked, "How I am going to handle this?" I literally heard God say, "You're not. I am."

Even with this confirmation and with my pastor praying so earnestly, my faith as a Christian was wavering because of the fear of the unknown. I tried so hard not to get too emotionally involved; I tried to stay neutral. I would accept the fact if he lived with great joy, or if he had to go; I would accept that with pain and sorrow.

We had gone through so much that it began to put wear and tear on my family. At a time like this, you would think the family would stick together, but it seemed that the stress of pulling the plug took everyone for a great loop. I was afraid to leave the hospital; I wanted to spend every moment that I had with him because it might be my last.

The people in the intensive care unit were tired of seeing us because we were a very large family and we were in and out all day everyday for the two weeks that he resided there. My family would come one by one or two by two, but after a while everyone started arguing and people were saying things to each other that were not necessary or appropriate. It was a mess all the time. I didn't want to even be a part of the family by then. I thought if my father passed, then I was just going to travel, and my brother was so angry that he said, "I'm moving far away and I am never coming back. I'll stay in touch with the family by phone."

"The only problem with that is that we are such a close knit family," I told him. "Wherever you go, even if you run to the ends of the earth, your heart will be with you and you will long to see us and be with us again." I was going one way and my brother was going another and I had a sister who didn't know whether she was coming or going.

A Few Days before the Pulling
One night I went to bed suffering with anxiety so bad that my left arm had sharp pain in it, and felt funny. Then I began to have strange pains in my neck and chest, and my left pinky began to tingle. I tried to pray, but I was too nervous. I got up out of the

bed and went into the next room and got my daughter. I felt that if someone were with me I wouldn't be so afraid. But honestly I was beyond afraid, I was just plain scared. It became internal and was beginning to flow through my blood stream and really starting to hurt.

I called a friend knowing he was very tired, but I tried to keep him on the line anyway just so I wouldn't be alone. I knew that this was a job for Jesus and I needed him really bad. As I talked with my friend on the phone with a few silent pauses in between, I tried to close my eyes to relax. When I did, all I could see was the sadness as the time drew closer and closer to my father's plug being pulled.

I could hardly breathe just thinking about it.

God always has a way to lighten up the situation. My friend began to pray on the other line even though he was so tired. As he prayed, his words began to slur and it actually began to sound like he was speaking in another language. It was kind of funny to hear him try so hard to pray for me and for him to be in la-la land.

He was probably two seconds away from a deep snore and a few cows flying over the moon. I got a little laugh out of that, and it took my mind off of me for a little while. I hadn't slept in days and I began to regress back to a child. My simple prayer was, "Now lay me down to sleep, I pray the Lord my soul to keep; if I shall die before I wake, I pray the Lord my soul to take. Amen."

I finally got some sleep that night and headed for the hospital the next day to visit my dad. The day before the actual pulling we all began to sing songs to him. His favorite song was, "I Believe I Can Fly" and we began to sing the whole lyrics to him.

I believe I can fly,
I believe I can touch the sky,
I think about it every night and day
I spread my wings and fly away,
I believe I can soar
I see me running through that open door,
I believe I can fly, believe I can fly,
I believe I can fly, because I believe in miracles.

It was so beautiful, we all came together as a family and sang it in perfect harmony. It was quite sweet. He began squeezing our hands and we even got a little smile out of him. It was like my father was the mayor or something because he had so many visitors that day that it was unreal. The nurses didn't say much because we were very polite and we were always co-operative. They considered us a cool family. I thought that was very nice, and they were very considerate of our situation.

I always knew that my father was well liked, but this was unreal. There were lots of people who heard about my father being ill. I don't know how they got the news so quickly, but when you live in small town news travels fast. All I could say was, "Wow, how'd you hear the news that quick?" I was in shock. We hadn't even told anyone ourselves, because we had just gotten the news. So yes, when I say news travels fast I mean that literally.

There was an overwhelming response to my father being sick and I just want to say to everyone that made their way to see him: I appreciate it and thanks for all of your prayers because they certainly helped. Once again thank you all.

I See You

As I lay here next to you
I'm rubbing away your invisible tears
But today I see something
I see you crying
I feel your tears
Streaming down your soul
Lost for words
The moaning of your heart are being heard
Yes as I lay next to you
I wipe away your invisible tears
Without a single word being said
I hear you

The Day of the Pulling

We went to the hospital that day. Everyone was late, of course, because no one really wanted to show up. This was going to be it. It was either he was going to live today or he was going to die today. It was the day we had all been waiting for not to happen. We all went in the room and there were about 50 people to say their goodbyes.

The situation did not look very good, so we all got together with the doctor and went into the room. The doctor explained the whole procedure and then he took my father off of life support— he pulled the plug. We all stood and watched as my father began gasping for air. That's when Elders of my church began to pray, because honestly it was hard for me at that moment. My sisters and I began rubbing the top of his head and kissing his cheek.

We knew that there was nothing else that we could do for him, so we decided to sing to him in harmony. We sang his favorite song again, "I Believe I Can Fly." As he still kept gasping for air, his breathing got more and more shallow. We kept looking at his eyes rolling up in his head and his breathing would stop for about 45 seconds and then he would breathe again. This kept happening for about an hour.

We called the doctor into the room again and he said it shouldn't be long. He should be gone within half an hour. We were so hurt, but we didn't want him to die alone. We wanted to support him in his death if he was going to die, and the way that it was looking, he was a dead man. As time passed, my dad kept looking like he was on his last breath, but another hour passed by and then another and another.

He was on morphine to ease the pain of death, but for some reason he was not dying. The doctors were amazed and so were we. They said he wouldn't make it through the night because of his breathing, so they put him into another room. It was quite cold and gloomy, but my sisters and I spent the night with him there. When morning came, he was still alive. It was unbelievable! I watched a real miracle right before my very eyes. That same day he was moved down to the third floor.

But something was wrong. He had suffered a stroke during the night and he couldn't talk or move his hands or legs. I called my pastor and she began to pray. Within a day or two, he was moving his hand and legs a little. He was still in another world, but he began to speak slowly. He couldn't eat because of the tubes that had been in his throat for two weeks, and for a week they couldn't get him to swallow anything. The next week, they scheduled him for surgery to put a peg in his stomach and on that same day he decided to begin to eat.

Within a couple of weeks my father was home. I had him hold a ball in his hand to get full use of it again. It was hard for him to hold a fork, but I kept speaking life into his spirit. I kept telling him positive things; I told him he could do it. He kept trying to walk, but it was hard for him. He was paralyzed, but that never stopped him from trying. It seemed as though my father had gone to heaven and come back with some information from God for us.

My father went back and forth into the hospital for the next few months. He and I began to discuss his going home to be with God. I told him, "If you get to heaven before I do, I need you to do three things for me. I need for you to come and let me know that you made it and that you're OK. And please tell my mother and my brother that I love them and that I miss them dearly. And please ask God to speed up the process of my career and my finances." Dad said that he would work on that for me.

As we spoke, he was smiling. He was very excited about meeting my mother and brother again. One thing I love about my father is, if there was anything that he could do for me, he would, no matter what. I had only a few requests, and he was going to try to do just that for me.

Some Unexpected Hilarious Moments

After my dad came home from the hospital, he was very fragile so we needed to watch his every move. One day the telephone rang and my father decided in his own mind that he should answer the phone with the remote control. When I saw the remote control placed on his ear and he answered "Hello," I was no good for the rest of the day. It was the funniest thing I had seen since he had been sick, and I needed a good laugh. As I watched him say hello, he became a little agitated that no one on the line was responding to him. I heard him mumble something under his breath, but I couldn't quite catch it. I did detect a small attitude when he slammed the remote control down onto the arm of the chair as if he was putting it on the hook.

The next time the phone rang, I answered it for him. I couldn't allow him to continue to make me laugh that way, it just wouldn't be right. Later on that week, I noticed that the remote control began to play another roll: my father was brushing his hair with the buttons of the remote. He had his eyes closed and was stroking his hair gracefully and confidently from one side of his head to the other. I feel like he knew that he looked good and that was all that mattered.

What I've realized about life is that sometimes we look for the big things to make us happy or to make us laugh and then God allows something so little like this to take the edge off of things.

My advice for us all is to remember that good things do come in small packages. Just because it's small doesn't mean that it isn't good, because that laugh lives on in my life forever, if I need a little chuckle.

Philippians 4:8 says: "Finally brethren, whatever things are true, whatever things are noble, whatever things are just, whatever things are pure, whatever things are lovely, whatever things are of good report, if there is any virtue and there is anything praiseworthy, meditate on these things." Think on the good things that you have and don't dwell on the things that you don't have. My father still had enough life in him to be home with us a little while longer. I think on those things and I feel very blessed.

My Daddy's Death

It was New Year's Day of 2005 when I got the call that my father had passed away. The funny thing was that I was sitting in my room and I had heard a weird noise that got my attention. I looked over and I saw two beings that appeared to be running through my room holding hands. The first thought that came into my head was Mom and Dad. Don't tell me that the man that I know as Superman is finally going to rest in peace. No, is it so? Is he gone? I had had a dream a month prior in which my brother called me and said, "Daddy's gone."

It was like I was sitting there waiting for the phone call. The phone did ring, but it was my daughter J'nai and she was telling me that she had a dream last night that my father had died. I said, "Hummm." I was preparing to lie down to take a nap and the phone rang again. This time it was my brother and he said, "Missy, I think he's gone." After about three seconds he said, "Yeah, he's gone."

"I knew it, I just knew it." I told him. I hung up with him and I felt I needed to be sure. Even though I knew in my heart, I had to hear it from someone else. I called the house back and spoke to my brother's wife and I ask her if he really was gone and she said, "Yeah, he is."

When my dad died, I called Jay and asked him where he was. He said that he was just getting off the exit, that he would be right there. I pulled myself together and I drove up to my father's house. I walked in without fear and when I saw Jay standing there, the very first thought I had was, "I sure am glad that he is here." I felt like it gave me courage to face the situation. I didn't want to be alone at a time like that.

I looked at my father with his mouth slightly opened with no air coming out. I reached out and touched him and he was very warm. So I climbed up into the bed where he lay and I began to talk to him and I let him know that I had seen him with my mother, that I knew he was OK. I told him I loved him and began to kiss him on the cheek. I never thought that I would ever kiss a dead person and for the dead person to be the closest thing to me, my father.

I hadn't even been able to look at my mother when they pronounced her dead in the hospital room after she had a heart attack and flat-lined on the living room floor. That was the hardest thing for me to do and now two years later, Daddy was gone, too. Nobody ever told me that this was going to be easy. And guess what? It's not.

The worst thing about my dad dying was that I was his everything. My life was a very busy one, but he was a big part of my day. If he called, I came. If he needed me I was there. If he didn't need me I was still there—hospital visits, ice cream runs, good conversation. We had the best relationship that any father and daughter could have. All that was suddenly gone.

My life was very full in God, but empty without my father. I would drive uptown to go to all my activities and I would always just want to stop and see my dad, and he wasn't there anymore.

No more ice cream. No more seeing him in his car at the corner store. No more phone calls every day—and I mean every day. No more having him to turn to when I needed a friend.

My father really loved his children, but he and I had a special bond. I'm glad that he was my father and not some other family's dad. I am blessed to be a part of his blood. I will never forget my father. I had a very hard time getting over the fact that my father will never be around anymore. I always thought that if someone were really sick, their death would take away all the worries about their suffering—and all the pain that they suffered and all the pain that we suffered watching them suffer. I found out that it was actually worse for me, only because my father and I were so close.

Not only did I lose a sick parent, but I lost my friend, too.

How that makes my heart ache! I didn't know that it would be this hard. One good thing that did come out of the situation was that God placed a nice guy in my life to ease some of the pain. During my father's illness and death, he stood by me like a soldier stands by his belief in his country. He never left me high or dry.

I prayed a lot also. God is so good; he never leaves you comfortless. He will always have something or someone to help you through tough times. You might not see it, but if you look real close, he has blessed you with cats, birds, dogs or just anything that he thinks you need to make it. Not so easy, but not so hard that you can't bear it. I have my good days and then I have my bad days. I allow myself to grieve and not beat up on myself if I need to shed some tears. It was a loss. I lost a great man: my father.

Heads up, Dad. I know that you are flying without wings. You were a paratrooper and you used to jump out of airplanes, but now the wings that you have won't ever break nor bend, they will never need repairs, nor will you ever need to be in danger of any pain or suffering. You are and always will be a trooper in my eyes and in my life. Your memory lives on in my heart and I see you in my dreams all the time. Every once in a while, I take out a moment of silence in remembrance of you and I cry. I just want to let you know that you are worth every tear that I shed. I love you and I will never forget you or your favorite ice cream—butter pecan.

Behind Closed Doors

Behind closed doors
No one even knows my name
Heck sometimes I don't even
Know who I am myself
Grief just eating me alive
Don't like this feeling, ya know
I like being in control
Of my feelings
Who is this new person?
That has taken over me
You don't make me feel good
Grief, why do you even exist
Is it to build me?
Or just to tear me down
Why are you here
Why are you even around
Why is it that you make me
Hurt so bad?
Come on, you know the song
Why am I feeling sad?
Well it's beyond feeling sad
I have a hole in my heart
Now everything I think of
Just drops to the pit of my stomach
I'm so filled with grief and pain
That I need no food
Because there is no room for it
It's like gluttony

It's spilling over inside of my being
Please grief, try to be a friend
To me
Just look how I'm feeling
And please just loose me
I can't do this thing anymore
I see why people are drawn to
Bridges and they just want
To jump
Or to a bottle of pills
To stop the pain
Of the heart thump
But I hear a voice saying
Don't do it
I'm here
But I say
Grief hurts so bad that
If the devils don't kill you, the pain will
Oh God my redeemer
Will it ever end?
He says yes
Will it ever go away?
He says yes
Please God just make the pain go away
For me
He said I will
Please make it go away
He said okay I will
Just make it all go away
He said okay I did
One day when I wasn't thinking
It all went away

Apple Butter II

Guess what! I finally bought a jar of apple butter. The day that
I bought it, I wasn't in any pain. It didn't hurt me at all. I bought it
at a time when I was feeling very cheerful. I was out shopping for

my daughter's surprise party and I ran across a jar, and by then the sting of pain was gone. I have not eaten it yet, but I am glad that I made a step in the direction.

I'll never forget you and I will always love you, Mommy.

Just My Thoughts Again

I've often heard the song, "Nobody Ever Told Me that the Road Would Be Easy." But, Lord, no one ever told me that life was going to be this hard either. Boy, life's experience will teach you a thing or two or three or four.

CHAPTER 14

I Met a Man

I was a very busy person—traveling doing plays, making music, and pursuing an acting career in New York City as a single mom. I was also very active in my local church. Once, while traveling, I went to Schenectady where my church had been invited to sing one evening at the church of a friend of my pastor.

There were a lot of musical selections, including a special guest group called God's devoted, which was headed by Jay Williams. After they performed their first song, Jay came off of the drums and talked about the group and the songs they were going to perform that evening. In the midst of this, he asked if the church could pray for his mother because she was in the hospital and wasn't doing well at all. He said that his father had died just a few months ago, and as he tried to finish his sentence, he broke down and cried. Through his tears, he said that his father was gone and he didn't want his mother to die.

There was not a dry eye in the house. His heart was hurting and we all felt his pain. I felt it because I had just lost my mother two months prior. When he finished speaking, he sat back down on the drums and played them with great power and anointing. I had never seen anyone play like that and I was very impressed.

When church was over, he and I ended up standing next to each other. I can't remember who spoke first, but I clearly recall that we complimented one another. He told me that I had a powerful voice and I told him that I loved the way that he played drums. My friend leaned over and said he was cute, but I never thought twice about it because I had just been dumped by a member of my church, and that night I had to watch him and his new girlfriend sitting in front of me laughing and chatting just like I wasn't even there. So I was too angry to think about anyone being cute.

After that service, two years went by and I hadn't thought

about him except when my friend would ask, "Remember that cute guy from Schenectady?" I would reply, "Oh yeah, the guy that was upset about his mom."

One day I was talking to Artie and Nita, who had joined our church in Kingston, and Nita told me that she was related to the Williams up in Schenectady. "Do you have a real cute cousin whose father had passed away and his mom was sick?" I asked. She replied, "Yes, that's Jay." I ask her how he was doing and how his mother was. She told me that his mother had pulled through and they both were doing wonderful. I told her how my friend thought he was so cute, so she said she was going to invite him down to one of our services. I thought that was cool. I wasn't thinking about any type of relationship because I was entirely too wounded, Well, then again, I wanted to, but I was just too afraid. I was tired of being mistreated and didn't' want to experience that anymore in my relationships for love. I remember 6 months prior I walked into my house one from crying, I was wounded by someone I thought I loved; I was tired of being played. I felt as if my life of love was running the same ole cycle as the one before, being full of pain, I ran up the stairs to my room as I stripped off all of my clothes. I stood before the mirror, butt spanking naked, and I began to talk to God. My very words were, "God, I was born naked. Now, I come back before you naked. I can't handle these emotions that I am carrying anymore. I need you to take them from me and help me. I can't do this anymore." I lay on the floor crying my heart out, while still naked, for 45 minutes. I then got up, went into the bathroom, and got into the shower. I then said to God, "I need you to wipe away every illegal spirit that has attached itself to me." And as I put the soap on me, I imagined that the soap was the illegal spirits being washed away down the drain. When I finished, I got out of the tub, dried off, and I felt that a refreshing had taken place. I then went downstairs, stood in front of another mirror and I said these words, "God, you made Eve for Adam. Now, please make my husband for me." I then took my hands and stretched them up to God and said, "Now God, send my husband to me." I then told God what I wanted in my husband. Then I heard Him tell me to pray for my husband every day. In the meantime, I began my new journey; believing that he was being prepared for me. I didn't have to pray every day, "God, send him to me." I just believed that he was being prepared for me, God put me on his mind, and we were going to meet soon.

As this was happening, different men began to approach me out of the blue and ask me out. I mean, guys from my childhood, old ex's and even a man riding a bike rode up on the side of me asking me out. That's when I knew that God was really up to something for me. I then began to focus on getting my spiritual life on the right track; not focusing on a man or anything but God.

I began bible study every Wednesday and prayer on Friday nights.

Well one Friday night at prayer in my time of being transformed the spirit of the Lord was high and my pastor (Pastor Armour) asked did anyone have any special prayer request. I said yes I do, I then said I am ready for my husband to come. Something happened at that moment it was like a divine connection. Something hit Brother Frank Elliot and he grabbed his stomach and began to run around the church hollering, The spirit of God hit my pastor and she began to speak in her heavenly language and I began to cry. I knew at that moment that something was good was going to happen to me pertaining to my husband coming for me. It was only us three there in the church and that's where the miracle took place. Well, fast forward. .

Two weeks later Jay and his friend Justin came into the church on Sunday. My daughter told me later that she had said to herself, "Wait until Mommy sees him and wait until he sees Mommy. He's the one."

My girls knew me, and they knew I didn't date. I barely gave a guy a chance to even say hello, because I thought that he might want more and I didn't have it to offer. Whoever was going to have me would have to really fight to get me. I was done.

When Jay and Justin came into the church that day, I was downstairs in the back room. My girls came down and said, "Mommy, someone's here to meet you." I said okay, and when I came out, there was Jay standing there with his cousin's children. They were smiling and all excited about his meeting me, but at the time I didn't know why. I found out later that Jay's cousin bought him there especially to formally meet me.

We greeted each other with hellos and smiles. We all went upstairs into the service and I had to go sing with my praise and worship team. Every once in a while I would look over at Jay and Justin and give them a little smile, just to say thank you for coming. Each time I looked over at him, I would see him laughing and talking to Justin. I even saw him fall over onto the bench once, covering his face but so full of laughter. I couldn't help but wonder what was making him and Justin crack up and laugh during service. Jay was looking around the church checking out his surroundings, but I did catch him staring at me a few times during the rest of the service.

After church, Jay didn't hesitate to make his way up to where I was sitting in the choir stand. He just stared at me for a moment; he looked a little dazed. Then he said, "I didn't know that you could sing like that. I love the way that you sing. Girl, I will marry you today."

I just looked at him like, "wow," and then I said I couldn't do that.

"Why not?" he asked. "They told me that you wanted to meet me."

"Who said that?" I asked.

"My cousins," he answered.

As we were sitting there, lots of people began to crowd us, so we left that conversation alone for a while. I asked him to hold on for a moment, that I needed to ask my pastor something, but I would be right back. I watched him watch me as I walked off. I smiled at him and he already had a smile on his face.

I walked into the pastor's office and before I could say anything, she said to me, "That is your husband." I looked at her like, "No, he couldn't be," and she said, "I don't know when or how, but that man down there is going to be your husband."

A big part of me wanted to believe her, but I have had so many people speak things to me that never happened that I had a fear that no one could love me for real. Even though God had let me know ahead of time, it still scared me. I knew that my pastor wouldn't lie to me and I did trust her on the things that she said, but I just didn't want another let down.

But she was right.

I came back down stairs with the words that she had spoken to me in the back of my mind. I walked over by Jay and Justin and asked them what they were doing after church. They said that they were going over to Artie and Nita's house. Jay asked me what I was going to do after church, and I told him I don't know, that I'd ask my friend what she was going to do. She said that her husband was waiting outside to take her out to dinner. I was going to be alone with these two guys that I didn't even know. My friend had been the one who said he was cute and now she was ditching us for dinner. I thought that was kind of cute. I told her to go ahead and I would hang out with them for a while.

So we went to his cousin's house and being the friendly person that I am, I just entertained them for a little while. He asked, "Why'd they tell me that it was you that I was coming to see?"

"I don't know," I admitted. "Your cousin and I talked about my friend, who thought you were cute and that you should come down."

"That's not what they told me," he insisted.

I think they had their own agenda. Maybe they were hoping that we would get together, because when they brought Jay to the church, they were all excited and smiling when they reintroduced me to him. Since he had come all the way down in good faith, I knew that we could make the best of our visit.

I was left alone with both guys, but that was no real problem for me as I knew how to handle people. When it was time to go, Jay asked for my phone number, and I gave it to him along with one of my CDs. Jay went back to Schenectady and I went back to my normal everyday life.

Jay still had eyes for me and was not giving up, we began to talk on a professional basis. We were both into music and each of us was very interested in what the other was doing. Lo and behold, he and the guy who came down with him on that first trip began visiting our church a little more. They would come over for dinner and just hang out like we had known each other forever.

As the friendship progressed and he needed someone to talk to, I began to give him sound counsel. He began to open up about everything, and I mean everything, and me being who I am began to shed some light on his situation with a little humor and I let him know that we have all sinned and fallen short of the glory of God. I shared some of my downfalls in life and let him know how God bought me out and redeemed me through His blood.

As the process kept on going and going, I felt a little funny that we were connecting so well. He was like me and I was like him all the way down to how we eat. My friend told me, "I believe in my heart that he was meant to be with you." It's funny that she would say that because his pastor took one look at me and told Jay that I was going to be his wife. That made three major people speaking into our lives, along with the people who tried to set us up.

"Maybe I had to see Jay for you because you couldn't see him for yourself," she suggested. "At the time that we first met him, you weren't looking at anyone because your mom had just died. And two months prior to that, the guy that you were talking to dumped you for another woman, and it just so happened they were at the same service with us that night."

She was saying that I had been pre-occupied with my past. She added, "It probably could have happened for you that night at the service, but he was crying because his father had just died and his mother was in the hospital. It was not a good time for either of you. God sent him to you and this is the way that he had to do it. I believe that he is the one."

"Are you sure?" I asked.

"Yes, girl, I am for sure," she assured me.

Jay and I continued to keep our relationship as business and a friendship for a very long time—until one day I realized I had feelings for him.

The Relationship Began to Grow

How is it that everything that I wanted in a man was all wrapped up in him, you know nothing ever comes easy. Jay and I were getting closer and closer, I couldn't help but to think is he the one. Every time I turned around he was right there. He would travel, an hour to see me every chance that he got. Why? What did he see in me that made him travel like that? I know that I am a sweet woman, but this sweet? I never had anyone make such a fuss over me.

Guys had wanted to take me out, but because of the few relationships that didn't work, it was hard for me to really give anyone a chance. Even this guy, because I figured that he was going to be just like the rest—sneaky, unfaithful, and all the other unorthodox things that go with bad relationships.

As the relationship progressed, I began to feel like everything was going to be all right. We took it one day at a time, with me still feeling insecure and all. The one thing that I could appreciate about him was that he understood me, even before I opened my mouth. He could sense when I was uncomfortable, hurt or just even bothered by something.

One thing that I really liked about myself in my learning was that I didn't change to please him; I was able to be myself. He loved wrestling, I hated wrestling but I didn't sit around and pretend it was my favorite just to please him. I needed to be me and he needed to be him.

Another thing I liked was that when I had doubts or questions, I was always able to be me and ask, with no hesitation. I knew "it's not what you say, it's how you say it," and I was considerate of his feelings during my interrogation. Sometimes some things are better left unsaid. As the relationship went on, things began to get much better. I was able to be more comfortable with him and we began to work things out. Communication was our biggest friend.

The thing that touched me the most was that my father, before he died, wanted to meet this young man and ask him questions about what kind of plans he had for me. Jay would come down from Schenectady and visit my sick father with no complaints. He never lied to my father or to me. If he said that he was coming, he came. My father and he began to build a relationship and it really became tight. He even came to church with my father a month before he passed away.

That was my father's first time at my church ever. And my father had always promised me that he was going to come, and he did. Not only did he come, but he came with the man that I love now. It was sweet to look in the back of the church and see the man that I loved with everything within me and the man that I was in love with sitting right next to him. I'd never had a feeling like that before. I knew that my father loved me so much that he didn't want to leave me all alone, that he had to make sure that I was going to be taken care of before he left.

When he met Jay, I believe that he was ready for heaven. Because he knew that after I had taken care of him and all of the stuff that I had been through, that Jay would take me to heaven and back, right here on earth.

My dad knew that Jay would be good to me, and honestly, he is nothing but good to me, which makes it very easy for me to be very good to him. I began to realize that God had made him just for me.

I was very happy when it all hit me that he was out for my good and not for my bad. He was just everything that I wanted and then some. He began to smother me with love and in return I wanted to bear my soul to this man—no holds barred. I wanted to know everything about him and he wanted to know me. We learned each other's ways and without argument, it all worked out to where we are today—in love.

I always say that if you try to out love one another, you will never fall out of love. My heart is overwhelmed right now. I am full of him. Everything in my being calls out "Jay."

When I sleep, I sleep Jay, and when I wake I want to see Jay. I love the way that he loves me. Lots of times in my life I would give of my love to people and they would take it for granted. They didn't understand my love for nothing so they took it for nothing. Jay wants my love and he believes in my love, it is not a one-sided thing, it is two-sided. Just as he wants my love, he desires to please me, so he desires that I desire him for the love that he displays. I can honestly tell you it is not hard to love a man like that. If I am hurt, he hurts, If I get cut then he bleeds. It is so perfect that it's almost scary, but I'm going with the flow of it. I will not throw my love away. I will keep him and cherish him always.

You want to hear something kind of funny? I am such a nice

and giving person, and once someone said to me, "You are too kind. You should stop being so nice to people. People are just taking your kindness for granted." So I prayed and asked God to send me someone who would fit the type of person that I am. I didn't want to change. This was the way God made me and I was perfectly happy with me.

Well, what did God do? He sent me someone just like myself; I was allowed to be myself without changing for that person. If I were to change my good habits for someone, I wouldn't be me. As T.D Jakes said, I would be a carbon copy of someone else and not a great original of myself. I said all that to say this: he loves me and guess what? So do I.

Not Just My Thoughts

God told me to find love, joy, peace and happiness in Him and when a good man does enter into my life, he will be an asset to our love.

The Man I Met Proposed

Oh, my goodness, who would have ever thought. Not me in a million years. I can't believe all of the things that I have gone through, and all the things that I acquired through other people's obstacles, and now I am getting married. It's almost like, "Why or how could this good thing be happening to me?" And he has the nerve to be good looking and—oh, my goodness again—full of intelligence.

Let me tell you the story about this young man that is blessing my soul every day. I always wanted to be married. Jay and I began talking to each other in May and less than a year later, he recognized that I was the marrying type. I thought that was good, because I have been treated pretty badly in my life—but enough of that.

He took me down to Virginia Beach for Valentine's Day weekend and he and his cousins took me out and showed me a great time that week. Then on February 15, they decided to take me to Ocean View Beach in Virginia, at 11:30 at night, overlooking the tunnels of love. When we got there, I saw a sign in the sand that said forever and ever and ever. I thought it was cute. Jay and I were standing toward the water and his cousins were standing looking at the water with their girlfriends when out of the clear blue, Jay asked, "What would you say"—then he turned me around and dropped to his knee—"if I ask you to marry me?"

I couldn't believe he was on his knee for me. I felt my knees getting weak and I fell to the sand with him. "Are you for real?" I asked. And he said, "Yes, I am!"

Finally, after gathering myself together, I said "yes." Then I began screaming at the top of my lungs, and, yeah, that's a lot of lung space! I jumped up and down and said to his cousins, "You knew this all along." They said, "No, Jay kept this a secret."

We set the date for June 18ᵗʰ 2005 and soon were planning the wedding. I know that my parents are in heaven smiling down on me. I know that my father wouldn't have died unless he saw something in the future that would make me happy. And sure enough, I couldn't be any happier than this. My New Year started off kind of rough, but by the next month, I was on Clouds 9, 10, and 11. I was feeling all right in my soul. I had a man that loved me, which was my father and now I have a man that is in love with me, and that's Jay.

Now I Am So Happily Married

I sat still a while and I waited patiently for God. I had been praying six months before I actually got to lay eyes on this beautiful man. I began to call him down into my loins, I asked God to take care of my husband-to-be before I even met him. I prayed for his arrival before he was even being packaged for me.

I was very lonely for quite some time. I had a big window in my apartment complex overlooking the bridge, which was quite beautiful. I always watched the fireworks from the window. The kids always wanted to go to the festivities and I allowed them to go every year with friends. I stared out of that big window alone for years. I would cry some years because I just wanted to be with someone who really loved me. I was tired of being by myself. We are made to love, not be all alone forever.

After God sent Jay to me, we were married June 18, 2005, I

didn't think about it, but the Fourth of July was right around the corner. I went from no husband for years to having one sitting right next to me. I began to cry, and he asked me why I was crying. I told him that from this very window, I had prayed for him to come to me; from this very room I asked God to allow me to share my every dream with the love of my life. I had just realized at that very moment that God had given me the desire of my heart. I told my husband that he had filled my desire by just answering a simple prayer of the Fourth of July.

My husband wiped my tears and told me from now on it would always be the Fourth of July for us. He held me tightly for a long time, promising that from now on I would only have tears of joy. Then he lifted my head up and kissed me. We watched out the window for a while and then we proceeded to make our own fireworks…ahhhhhh, I sure can appreciate the sweet joys of life.

We have been growing more and more in love as the days go by. This is the best relationship that I have ever been in. I have never had a man love me so much, and he does things for me that no other would have done, or could have done. He is beyond the man of my dreams; he is the man of my eternity. Our love will flow forever. I didn't think I could love anyone this way, or that anyone could love me the way he loves me. I have never seen it, nor experienced it. I can't say it enough: I love the way my husband loves me.

We have an easy going kind of love that flows gently; we understand each other with ease. I could never begin to thank God enough for my husband. He prays for me; he lays hands on me when I need it. He is a powerful man of God that allows God to have his way in his life. He is a loving father, and a wonderful friend. God sent me someone who is full of laughter and loves to have fun. We were two separate people going different ways with the same vision. God caught him by the leg and caught me by the foot, and after the spiritual surgery was done he put us on one path. We have been together now 11 years and it only gets better and better. I allowed myself to love and I allowed myself to be loved. This has been more than I could ever ask for and I am so ever grateful to our powerful God who not only answers prayers but he also answers desires.

God, I could have never done anything like this. You filled my life and my dreams. You sealed this deal and I just want to say thank you for loving me and breaking me off a piece of your heart through your servant man, my husband. God thanks a whole lot bunch much...lol.

It's you!
When I'm at work, I think of you
When I'm at home, I think of you
When you're near me, I think of you
When we evolve into one, I thank you
When I'm on the go, I'm with you
When I'm sitting still, I'm with you
When we're apart, I 'm with you
When I'm with you, I'm with you
When I'm lost in thought, I love you
When I have no thoughts at all, I love you
When there's you there's me, I love you
When there's me there's you, I love you
When I hurt, I need you
When I cry, I need you
When I laugh, I need you
When is there ever a time that I won't need you
When I see you, I want you
When I don't see you, I want you
When I daydream, I want you
When I want you, I want you
When I'm excited, I call your name
When I'm speaking of you, I call your name
When lying next to you, I call your name
When God called me, he also called your name

In Conclusion
No matter what you are going through or what it looks like, don't ever give up on your dreams, because if I had given up, you wouldn't be reading this book right now. Make your dreams come

true by putting time into you and being true to yourself.
    Out of all of my hurts I share with you,
    out of all of my pain I sing to you,
    and out of all of my grief, I write to you,
    out of a pure heart I pray for you,
    and out of a broken spirit, I feel you too.
    Out of all that I have been through,
    I know what you're going through.
    If I didn't know at the time
    the reason why it all had to happen,
    now I know, because reader,
    I am here just for you.
    You can make it and you will make it.
    No matter what the weapon is
    that forms against you,
    just tell yourself that it may sting you,
    it may even hurt you, but overall,
    it can never take or touch your soul.
    The weapon that has tried
    to come up against you
    shall and will not prosper.
    I know now that I am more than a conqueror.
    Through Christ Jesus who lives within me,
    I made it through every test
    and through every storm.
    Though I've been ripped and I've been torn,
    when they knocked me down,
    God picked me up,
    when they talked about me,
    God loved me still,
    when they hurt me,
    He lifted me,
    and when they cursed me,
    it was God who blessed me
    and I made it.
    I made it.
    I made it.

And so can you....

My Great Life Today

Today, I am a very happy woman who has over-come many fears, pain, hurt, and betrayal. Everything you can name that has to do with hurt, I've suffered. I have given myself a pat on the shoulder and said, "You have done a great job turning your life around." I have allowed God to reform me into His soldier. When I went into the battle, I couldn't see all of the darts and arrows thrown at me; but, by the time I got done with training, I came out strong with lifted shoulders and my head held high. God has blessed me with a wonderful husband who has my back like none other. I have finally found the love I was in search of. But more importantly, I have found myself. That's when I was able to love freely. The most important things in life are to know who you are and to understand that you are not what people say you are even if you've made mistakes. God gave you a name and He gave you a purpose. Follow through on what God has for you and you can't go wrong. I smile so much now that you would never know I suffered one day of my life. To tell you the truth, I don't even understand the peace that is in my life now. Happy is a place where I love to hang out. I love to have the freedom to just enjoy life. I go on long walks. I love long talks with the ones I love. I love the short and long kisses my husband gives me every morning and evening (and anytime in between). God has given me a peace that surpasses all man's understanding. Philippians 4:7. Today, I smile at the sun rising, the rain falling, the dogs barking, the cat meowing, and the birds chirping. I have just fallen in love with life and life alone. My passion is to let everyone know that with God all things are possible. I am a living witness and I live by these very words.

Letter from Christine

For two true leaders

When I think of Missy and Jay, I see two people who went from nothing to a whole lot of something. They are two beautiful individuals that love Christ wholeheartedly. They both withstood lots of abusive pain the kind that makes you want to go insane. But they both kept struggling to do what's right not giving up the in the fight. Two dedicated members of their church, who are defiantly about God's work. God knew their needs, wants and likes and he helped join them together as one in Christ, In which they now share compassion, forgiveness and love in a new light. They are true and a living testimony as to what I believe Christian couples should be. So I want to say thank you Missy and Jay for being all that you can be and for helping open up closed doors for a lost soul like me.

I love you both like cooked food,

Love, your baby sister Christine

Letter from Patricia

When I look at my brother this time his smile is real and sure. He has found a true love who he can depend on and one who he believes in. When I see the two of them, they show me that love can be pure and honorable. With their love for each other and the gleam and sparkles in their eyes show me that real love in a marriage can forever be found if your mate is your friend and your lover, with trust in your hearts for each other you can make it.

When I look at the two of them, I see love and happiness and a life full of joy, elevations in ministry and healing for girls and boys. When I look at the two of you, your smiles say so much more. A love everlasting that we can all adore,

With love to the both of you,

Your sister Pat

CPSIA information can be obtained
at www.ICGtesting.com
Printed in the USA
FFOW03n2130031215
19201FF